BUILDING A MINISTRY
OF SPIRITUAL
MENTORING

OTHER BOOKS BY
DR. JAMES GRASSI

Guts, Grace, and Glory

The Ultimate Men's Ministry Encyclopedia

A Study Guide of Israel

Crunch Time

Crunch Time in the Red Zone

Wading Through the Chaos

The Ultimate Hunt

In Pursuit of the Prize

Heaven on Earth

The Ultimate Fishing Challenge

The Spiritual Mentor

Men's Ministry Catalyst Website:
www.mensministrycatalyst.org

BUILDING A MINISTRY OF SPIRITUAL MENTORING

BY JIM **GRASSI**

Thomas Nelson
Since 1798

NASHVILLE   DALLAS   MEXICO CITY   RIO DE JANEIRO

Published in Nashville, Tennessee, by Thomas Nelson. Thomas Nelson is a registered trademark of HarperCollins Christian Publishing, Inc.

Page Design and layout: Crosslin Creative

Images: Jim Grassi, Dana Grassi, Catherine Mullaney Kmac, istock.com, and VectorStock.com

Thomas Nelson, Inc. titles may be purchased in bulk for educational, business, fund-raising, or sales promotional use. For information, please e-mail SpecialMarkets@ThomasNelson.com.

Unless otherwise noted, Scripture quotations are taken from the New King James Version. © 1982 by Thomas Nelson, Inc. Used by permission. All rights reserved.

Scripture quotations marked The Voice are taken from The Voice™ translation. © 2012 Ecclesia Bible Society. Used by permission. All rights reserved.

Scripture quotations marked NIV are taken from the Holy Bible, New International Version®, NIV®. Copyright © 1973, 1978, 1984 by Biblica, Inc.™ Used by permission of Zondervan. All rights reserved worldwide. www.zondervan.com

ISBN: 9781401677930

Printed in the United States of America

14 15 16 17 18 RRD 5 4 3 2 1

CONTENTS

FOREWORD

Approximately fifteen years ago God called me to form a ministry team in northern Idaho. Because of what I had seen in most churches, I knew I wanted something different for my church. I felt that for many Christians church had become a one-hour Sunday experience that had no carry-over impact in their lives and families throughout the week.

God gave our team a vision to establish a church that evolved into four basic elements to creating a disciple-making culture within our congregation.

First, the messages would be prepared from God's Word, and entertaining people was not a priority. Secondly, we would endeavor to create small groups that really cared for people and promoted relational discipleship. Next, we wanted to intentionally connect with our community by developing a compassionate program of serving others. And finally, we would create a strong dynamic men's culture. If you get the men, you will get the entire family.

Jim Grassi has been a friend for years as well as a part of the team here at Real Life Ministries. Jim helped us in the beginning to create a movement that attracted men and encouraged them to be the spiritual leaders in their homes, churches, and communities. His heart isn't just for them to come to know Christ, but to help them become authentic spiritual mentors to others. Dr. Grassi desires to make disciples who can make disciples.

Over the years the Lord has led Jim and his ministry team (Men's Ministry Catalyst) to develop proven strategies and resources that have successfully helped churches develop vibrant men's ministry programs. *Building a Ministry of Spiritual*

Mentoring is an outstanding contribution that will assist churches with biblical thinking, practical tools, and innovative resources that empower men while challenging them to become disciple-making mentors. I am pleased to suggest that leaders of churches not only read this book but adopt his strategies into your ministry. The ministry he leads is helping churches all around the United States, and it can help yours too.

What an amazing thought. What if men represented Jesus to the world by playing the part that God designed them to play in their marriages, homes, and churches? The result would be marriages that last and kids who can withstand the pressures of the world. The result would be changed churches that change whole communities.

Slowly but surely we could see a change even in our culture—one man at a time. Men's Ministry Catalyst and this book can help you start that movement right where you are.

> Pastor Jim Putman
> Author, international speaker, and founder of
> Real Life Ministries

✳ ✳ ✳

Pastor Jim Putman is the founder of Real Life Ministries, identified as one of the fastest-growing and largest churches in the United States, despite the fact that it is located in a sparsely populated area. He is a noted author of several books on discipleship.

INTRODUCTION

OUR CALLING

But you be watchful in all things, endure afflictions,
do the work of an evangelist, fulfill your ministry. For
I am already being poured out as a drink offering, and
the time of my departure is at hand. I have fought
the good fight, I have finished the race, I have kept
the faith. Finally, there is laid up for me the crown of
righteousness, which the Lord, the righteous Judge,
will give to me on that Day, and not to me only but
also to all who have loved His appearing.

—2 Timothy 4:5–8

"Fulfill your ministry" means "fulfill whatever God wants you to do." Timothy's ministry would not be exactly like Paul's, but it would be important to the cause of Christ. By kingdom standards, no God-directed ministry is small or unimportant. Whatever a man does for the cause of Christ is important.

Growing and dynamic churches seem to have four things in common: passionate pursuit of God, compulsive care for people, emphasis on home groups, and a strong and vibrant ministry to men. It is men who will lead the church to a new reformation. It is men who are accountable to strengthening families by modeling God's Word. It is men who can support and connect with assisting the widows (single moms) and orphans (41 percent of children with no biological father in the home)[1] of our day.

When sin came into the world, it was Adam who was standing and watching instead of proactively protecting and leading his family. How does the church inspire, equip, and deploy men for service? How can a body of believers be transformed into a dynamic ministry impacting communities for Jesus? What can be done to reach the majority of young men who no longer see their faith as an important part of their lives? What proven models exist to ignite men to serving our Lord and becoming participants in the life of the church instead of passive spectators? These questions and many more will be addressed in this book that will assist pastors, lay leaders, Christian colleges, seminaries, and para-ministries in developing dynamic partners who can minister to men.

A young preacher once complained to Charles Spurgeon, the famous British preacher of the 1800s, that he did not have as big a church as he deserved.

"How many do you preach to?" Spurgeon asked.

"Oh, about a hundred," the man replied.

Solemnly, Spurgeon said, "That will be enough to give account for on the day of judgment."[2]

Ministry should not be evaluated on the basis of statistics or what comments are made by members of a congregation after Sunday service. Disciples of Christ realize that service to God is about obedience to the principles established in Scripture and acknowledging the presence and power of the Holy Spirit in one's life. This was why Timothy was encouraged to be "watchful in all things" (2 Tim. 4:5) and carry on his ministry with seriousness of purpose.

Timothy was not only a preacher; he was also a soldier (2 Tim. 2:3–4) who would have to "endure afflictions" (2 Tim. 4:5). He had seen Paul go through sufferings on more than one occasion (2 Cor. 6:1–10; 2 Tim. 3:10–12). Most of Timothy's sufferings would come from the "religious crowd" that did not want to hear the truth. The religious crowd was also responsible for crucifying Christ and persecuting Paul.

"Do the work of an evangelist" would remind Timothy that all of his ministry must have soul-winning at its heart. This does not mean that every message or event should be a "sawdust trail, hellfire-and-brimstone" program. But it does mean that a messenger of God, no matter what he is doing, should keep lost souls in mind.

If while reading this book you get the impression that I'm frustrated with many churches in America, you are probably reading correctly. I intended to be a little critical about the way we are conducting church as related to involving men and specifically making disciples. For the most part, many of our churches have it wrong when they think about discipleship. Further, you might see some areas where I've painted a disturbing picture when it comes to identifying the current feelings of many men in our contemporary society.

For too long men have hidden their disappointments, failures, and frustrations. Due to trends within our culture and changes in the church itself, we find that too many men are leaving the church with no place to vent their frustrations and fears. To some degree and with over thirty years of experience in ministry to men, I will endeavor to expose some of our concerns and propose a number of ideas for the church to consider in developing a dynamic ministry to men within our churches and communities.

There should not be a loss of focus on simply entertaining others, but we need to constantly be thinking about those who do not know Jesus. The challenge Jesus gave His followers in Matthew 28 still holds true today:

> I am here speaking with all the authority of God, *who has commanded Me to give you this commission*: Go out and make disciples in all the nations. Ceremonially wash them through baptism in the name of the *triune God*: Father, Son, and Holy Spirit. Then disciple them. *Form them in the practices and postures that* I have taught you, and show them how to follow the commands I have laid down for you. And I will be with you, day after day, to the end of the age (vv. 18–20 The Voice).

A **MAN'S** MEANING AND **PURPOSE**

John was a typical guy who periodically attended church to keep his wife and family happy. When football season rolled around, you could find John sprawled out on his favorite recliner with a well-stocked TV tray tucked next to his chair. He felt that church lacked the energy and relevancy to the problems he faced. According to him, the church felt very feminine in its orientation, and nothing seemed very practical in helping him meet his daily challenges.

In the early 1990s, a unique and exciting moment among men caught John's attention. Promise Keeper (PK) rallies offered John something his church lacked. He felt this new men's movement addressed issues that connected with guys in a forum that both encouraged and challenged men.

After attending a PK event, John returned to his local church hoping to find that some of the principles taught at the rally would be carried over in the style of worship and programs at his church. Unfortunately, the pastor seemed more interested in winning a popularity contest than in discipling men. Despite

John's commitment at the PK rally, there did not exist a band of Christian brothers, a dynamic ministry to men, that would continue to educate, equip, inspire, and hold him accountable. Consequently, he soon went back to his everyday life without any further regard for seeking a deeper walk with the Lord.

Why do men fail to participate in poorly designed and implemented men's ministry programs? Is John any different from most men in the country? Typically, men do not respect, connect with, or support something that is doomed for failure. They can smell potential failure in the air. If the leaders of men's movements are not intentional about their ministries and have not carefully developed a pathway to success, there will be little buy in from men. Their time and resources will follow their passions and interests. Men typically avoid involving themselves in any activity that presents even the slightest potential for failure; we tend to measure life by how successful we are. And, in many cases, being "successful" means steering clear of disappointment. Thankfully, God values *significance* over *success.* For the spiritually mature man, there is tremendous freedom in knowing that because of Christ, men's failures can be forgiven and erased from God's memory. The true significance men have is found in Jesus, and in Him a man no longer has to fear failure.

> If the leaders of men's movements are not intentional about their ministries and have not carefully developed a pathway to success, there will be little buy in from men.

The dynamic tension within men is confusing as they explore "*who* they are" in comparison to "*Whose* they are." A wise intentional leader will develop strategic opportunities to help men see themselves as their heavenly Father views them. As men grow in God's love and acceptance, they will be transformed from being social or cultural Christians into true disciples of Christ Jesus (Matt. 13:22–23).

OUR CULTURE

Our nation continues to move toward what is known as a "fatherless society." One-third of children are born out of wedlock; twenty-four million kids don't live with their biological fathers; half of all marriages end in divorce. Fatherlessness is a rampant and well-documented problem in this society. Children who come from fatherless homes are five times more likely to experience poverty, emotional problems, teen pregnancy, and substance abuse. Fatherless children are also more likely to drop out of high school and experience problems with the law. It's no wonder that 85 percent of male prisoners report having had no father figure in their lives.[1]

The popular term "NASCAR fathers" describes an approach to parenting that is all too common in modern times. The image of a race-car driver roaring around the track at two hundred miles an hour, zipping into the pits for a super-quick oil change, then roaring off to rejoin the race with just a wave good-bye to those who keep him on track—this is just too close to what fatherhood looks like in many homes in America today. There is certainly a cost to the men who live this way, but the greater cost, in my opinion, is paid by the wives and children of such NASCAR fathers. A man who makes a quick "pit stop" at home, on his way between commitments and work, is not being a godly husband or father. God wants men to be husbands and fathers *first*, and good providers second. When a man switches these priorities, he does damage to himself and to others around him.[2]

I tend to agree with Pat Morley on most things. Much like his Man in the Mirror organization, Men's Ministry Catalyst seeks to be trend-setters when it comes to assisting churches in developing ministry to men. Pat said it well when speaking about fathers:

> We have become a nation of spiritual widows and practical orphans (James 1:27). These are real people—real casualties. As one police officer said, "Statistics are tragedies with the tears wiped away."
>
> Today's average man is like a deer caught in the headlights of a Hummer. He doesn't fully understand—and so can't apply—what God has to say about a man's identity, purpose, relationships, marriage, sex, fathering, work, money, ministry, time, emotions, integrity, and dozens of other subjects.
>
> As a result, most men are tired. They often have a lingering feeling something isn't quite right about their lives. Often their lives are coming unglued. And it is common for them to feel like nobody really cares. Even in the church, men are being left behind.[3]

Certainly, society is no friend to men. The media continues to play down the God-ordained leadership roles. Most sitcom television programs degrade men by portraying them as unmotivated and ignorant beings with little vision or passion for anything that is intellectual or spiritual. Men are seen as anything but complex and sophisticated.

In pondering this same issue, James, the half brother of Jesus, said, "Pure and undefiled religion before God and the Father is this: to visit orphans and widows in their trouble, and to keep oneself unspotted from the world" (James 1:27). Too many of us have been polluted by the world and are drowning in the cesspool of immorality and spiritual apathy.

Our ministry's research indicates that, if the senior pastors aren't committed to promoting and supporting dynamic men's programs, their churches will tend to grow slowly (if at all), and they will continually struggle with not having enough revenue to sustain their budgets. As mentioned in *The Promise Keeper at Work*, "When a child comes to faith, 9 percent of the time they can influence an un-churched family to become Christians. When a woman comes to faith in the same situation, only 13 percent of the time will her influence cause the family to come to faith. But when a man comes to faith, 93 percent of the time the entire family will come to faith and become participants in church."[4]

Steve Sonderman succinctly identifies some of the cultural challenges that men face and how the church can meet the greatest needs of men today:

> Let's see why men are ripe for harvest:
>
>> The American Male Is Friendless
>> The American Male Is Emotionally Isolated
>> The American Male Is Confused Over Masculinity
>> The American Male Is Success Driven
>> The American Male Today Is Spiritually Searching Building a Life-Changing Men's Ministry
>> What Are We Aiming For?
>> Men of Integrity
>> Men of Intimacy
>> Men of Identity
>> Men of Influence[5]

For the church, the issues our culture is facing provide unique opportunities to reach men. God has empowered the church to help ignite the passions and energies of men by addressing the spiritual and social problems of this age. To effectively minister to men, the church must help build a dynamic ministry to men by:

* Properly assessing and surveying the needs and interest areas of their men.

* Developing specific strategies and plans that stimulate involvement and commitment.

* Providing discipleship training and teaching programs that help men grow in their faith and develop a biblical worldview.

* Creating opportunities for men to identify and utilize their gifts and talents in their churches and communities.

* Reaching out to younger generations in creative ways.

* Encouraging men to minister together.

FAILURE OF THE CHURCH

The maze of liturgical thinking and formal ceremonies is contrary to what most men need and want in a worship experience. Books such as David Murrow's *Why Men Hate Going to Church*, Robert Lewis's *The Church of Irresistible Influence*, and Dudley Hall's *Men in Their Own Skin* helped me think about many of the reasons the modern church has failed to connect with men.

Not all church services alienate men, but many do. What makes a man feel intimidated in a worship service? I think three things contribute to intimidating men in church: they are paralyzed spiritually, feminized socially, and demoralized religiously.

Unfortunately, it seems like the general public, especially media and intellectual leaders, do not see Christianity as a

Six out of ten Americans
believe the church is irrelevant.

dominant social force in our country any longer. Instead, six out of ten Americans believe the church is irrelevant. And in the lives of the 170 million non-Christians in America (making our country the third-largest mission field in the world), that irrelevance provokes an ever-increasing cynicism and hostility.[6]

> **"Be culturally relevant."** According to this strategy, churches can best address their receding influence through contemporary repackaging. Unfortunately, this strategy often goes too far. It becomes relevance at the expense of substance. In many contemporary churches, believers no longer carry Bibles. Worshipers seek an experience with God minus the commitment. Therapy replaces morality. Entertainment crowds out the cross. Is it maturity we're after, or the "feel good"? "These new paradigm churches," David Wells says, "appear to be succeeding not because they are offering an alternative to modern culture, but because they are speaking with its voice and mimicking its moves." . . .
>
> "The average evangelical church in North America exists for itself," [Bill] Hull writes. "Churches are preoccupied with themselves, their routines, facilities, and filling their buildings for performances." Yes, men could certainly go there.
>
> Or, we realized, we could make a bold, radical move in a new direction. We could courageously pursue the type of church Jesus envisioned. . . .
>
> Without its own bridges to the world, church life—in time—fades into isolation, self-congratulation, and finally, irrelevance.[7]

Once again, the question is asked, "Why is it so important to reach men?" Who cares anyway? What difference does it make? The following statistics show the urgency in reaching men in our country:

✳ There are sixty-nine million men who make no profession of faith in Christ.

✳ Fatherless children are five times as likely to live in poverty, repeat a grade, and have emotional problems.

✳ Only one out of eighteen men in America are involved in active discipleship.

✳ As many as 70 percent of men have actively sought out pornography this year.

✳ Men make up 93 percent of all people incarcerated, and 85 percent of them have no father figure.

✳ As many Christians will divorce as non-Christians.

✳ Most men only know enough about God to be disappointed with Him.

✳ Too many men daily fight depression, loneliness, and despair with little hope to change their perspective.[8]

TRAITS OF SUCCESSFUL MINISTRY TO MEN

What does a successful ministry to men look like? Why do some churches seem to have a connection with men and their issues while other churches struggle? Churches that have successful men's programs share a number of traits that produce growth and spiritual transformation:

8

* Dynamic and innovative approaches to ministry

* Creative outreach opportunities

* Transparency of the leadership

* Risk-taking and adventurous in spirit and tasking

* Clear job descriptions for the leadership

* Seeing ministry to men as something that is affecting all the men of the church, not just those who show up for a monthly breakfast

* Men's council (leadership team) that shares the responsibility of leadership

* Pastor-led approach to discipleship and developing spiritual mentors

* Assessment tools that regularly measure the needs and concerns of the men

* Biblical approach to personal transformation that helps each man identify God's purpose and plan in his life

* Implementing proven programs, strategies, and curriculum from organizations like Men's Ministry Catalyst, Man in the Mirror, and Men's Fraternity

* Creating specific tasks for the men with time limitations to attract commitment

* Offering ministries that don't shame men into better parenting, but provide appropriate resources for spiritual growth

DOING EFFECTIVE MINISTRY TO MEN

Effectiveness requires intentionally using the time and resources necessary to develop and maintain a dynamic ministry to men. A group of guys meeting at a local diner once a week for Bible study does not constitute a vibrant men's ministry. Sponsoring a monthly pancake breakfast is also not the most effective way to disciple men.

Dynamic men's ministry is defined as an intentional effort of a church when it inspires men to implement disciple-making strategies so they may fully participate within and outside the church body. One important role of an effective men's ministry is equipping and encouraging men to be energized men of faith, effective community leaders, good husbands, and committed fathers. It is about reaching out to the un-churched with grace-filled hearts. Dynamic ministry to men includes engaging and challenging men to become active and supportive of one another.

When men become participants instead of spectators in their faith, they experience a spiritual vitality that reproduces itself in the lives of others. Discipleship becomes the end goal of relationships and spirituality. A joy-filled life becomes a primary by-product. Impossible, you say? Not at all! Our ministry regularly sees dynamic examples that we are reaching the majority of men within their churches. But this doesn't happen because a few good men wish it into existence. It happens when intentional leaders develop a specific strategy and action plan, and pray about engaging the men they directly influence. The tools, resources, ideas, and theology contained in this book will help you develop a dynamic ministry to men.

Dynamic men's ministry is defined as an intentional effort of a church when it inspires men to implement disciple-making strategies so they may fully participate within and outside the church body.

THE BLUEPRINT

When it comes to assembling things, men typically don't refer to the instruction manual or blueprint until after they have attempted to put the project together. And we're all familiar with the stereotype of men who will drive for miles before asking for directions. It's a "guy sort of thing" to equate asking for help with admitting that we don't know what we're doing or where we're going or that we are not in control!

Unfortunately, too many men's ministry leaders take the same approach when developing a dynamic men's ministry. From my vantage point, too many men's ministries fail due to the fact that no plan was developed, and, if developed, it wasn't followed. There appears to be a very high failure rate among pastors endeavoring to construct a dynamic men's ministry. In fact, in Exhibit 1-A I identify thirty-seven common failures that are typical of most discarded men's programs.

"Follow Me, and I will make you fishers of men" (Matt. 4:19). When Jesus presented that challenge to His followers, He didn't leave them without instructions. One can clearly see His plan for success in Matthew 6–8 and Romans 12. Jesus provided an instruction manual or blueprint for ministry and discipleship for all to follow. He believed in organization and detail. Christ empowered His followers with words *and* an action plan.

Jesus calls disciples to be transformers, or "revolutionaries" as George Barna calls them. Disciples are change agents willing to model Christ in every aspect of their lives. In order to do this, they need ministry leaders who are being transformed into spiritual mentors. Men don't need more entertaining programs, although they have their place; what men really need is committed leaders willing to be zealots for the cause of Christ. Committed men are needed who will step out and encourage other men to build relationships with the living God and with other men. George Barna has some challenging thoughts about men becoming more proactive about their faith.

> Spiritual transformation is any significant and lasting transition in your life wherein you switch from one substantial perspective or practice to something wholly different that genuinely alters you at a very basic level.[9]

And so it is with developing an effective ministry to men. In addition to the presence and power of the Holy Spirit, men must have a workable plan, effective strategies to achieve the desired goals, and the passion of a revolutionist. (See *The Spiritual Mentor* for more on this very important topic.)

MEN'S MINISTRY— DON'T TAKE IT FOR GRANTED

How hard can it be to minister to men? After all, men will accept anything. Or will they? Most churches seem to think that they have a good ministry to men if they have an early morning Bible study at a local restaurant, a monthly burnt pancake breakfast, and a prayer team. And then there are those who have reduced an effective program down to a simple five- or seven-step process. Most "quick-fix approaches" offer a variety of programs while giving little attention to the structure and process required for developing and sustaining a vibrant men's ministry. It is hard work; it is time-consuming—but it is absolutely worthwhile!

Some pastors or men's leaders reading this book would say, "We have a men's ministry. Isn't that enough?" One way to determine the value placed on a ministry is by looking at its place in the church budget. In 2001, the Christian church in America spent $31 billion representing 49.4 million members.[10] My experience in consulting with hundreds of churches reveals that the aver-age church has budgeted less than $1,000 per year for direct ministry to men.

The average church has budgeted less than $1,000 per year for direct ministry to men.

In comparison, substantial resources are spent on children and youth ministries. Yet, statistics tell us that 60–80 percent of church kids over eighteen will leave the church.[11] Why aren't churches investing in empowering, encouraging, and inspiring the husbands and fathers who are expected to lead and guide their families? How can a dad be expected to build a Christian legacy for his family if the church fails to provide resources and time to teach and equip him for the task of fatherhood? And where else could he possibly learn how to be a man of God if he is not taught by his parents? Certainly not in public school or through the media—it has to be the church.

Most men shoulder the responsibility of financially supporting a family, competing in a challenging work environment, becoming an involved husband and father, dealing with the temptations of the world, and exploring a growing relationship with God. They want and need a dynamic men's program that will strengthen their witness, help them overcome their guilt and shame, provide understanding and hope for their problems, and encourage them to form authentic and transparent relationships with other men.

TURBO-CHARGE YOUR MEN'S MINISTRY

What guy hasn't lived vicariously through actor Tim Allen's character Tim Taylor in his famous *Tool Time* moments, as seen on the television program *Home Improvement*? Tim was the master of modifying various tools and equipment to increase the power and effectiveness of the device he was working on. His obsession with "turbo-charging" power equipment seemed to resonate with his male audience who also desired to get the most out of everything.

A turbo-charged engine is a turbine-driven, forced-induction compressor powered by pressure from the engine's exhaust gas. To maximize the effect of turbo-charging, one can mix the air-flow with an appropriate amount of gasoline and nitrogen. This all adds more power, more efficient use of the machinery, and more fun for the driver.

A turbo-charged ministry to men is powered by the Holy Spirit in order to equip intentional leaders who are effective and dynamic men of God. They are leaders who promote opportunities for men to explore their deepest longings about faith and life. Turbo-charged ministries also want their men to seek a deeper relationship with their spiritual Dad, Abba Father, and one another. In addition to the traditional Bible studies, retreats, and pancake breakfasts, turbo-charged men's programs are filled with intentional opportunities for men to explore God's Word through relational experiences. When men come together for tasks such as assisting the elderly with chores, or helping single mothers, or participating in outdoor adventure programs, they have an opportunity to discuss matters at a deeper level. In his book *Wild at Heart*, John Eldredge clearly addressed the essence of what it takes to reach most men:

> Adventure, with all its requisite danger and wildness, is a deeply spiritual longing written in the soul of men. The masculine heart needs a place where nothing is prefabricated, modular, nonfat, zip lock, franchised, on-line, and microwavable. Where there are no deadlines, cell phones, or committee meetings. Where there is room for the soul. Where, finally, the geography around us corresponds to the geography of our heart.[12]

That is what ministry to men must be about. It must be a safe place where a guy can unpack his stored-up feelings, fears, failures, and aspirations. It must provide a venue for men to "get real" about the things in life that plague their souls and convict their spirits. It can be a brotherhood where men embrace one another as well as their gifts and talents. A great church supporting their men is a place where God the Father is promoted and true discipleship is explored.

More important than programs and events is a fellowship, a connection place, that turbo-charges men and promotes relationships. That brings us back to one of the fundamentals of the Christian faith: one brother helping another through the journey of life.

When men feel honored, respected, valued, nurtured, and energized by brothers who genuinely care for them, they become participants and not just spectators in the mission of the church. They are encouraged to become biblical role models in their homes, workplaces, and churches. Through the use of metaphors, anecdotes, parables, analogies, and even some humor, I want to encourage readers to become stronger in their faith by developing dynamic men's ministries that are turbo-charged by the power of the Holy Spirit.

BLUEPRINT FOR SUCCESS

I agree with Patrick Morley and other men's ministry leaders: if we, as the church, give men what they *need*, in the context of what they *want*, delivered in a system that *produces results*, we will have accomplished much. Many men's ministry leaders state that men want:

✳ A *cause* that they can give their lives to that will make a difference: a mission that has significance, meaning, and purpose

✳ A *companion* to share it with—relationships, love, wife, family, friends, and acceptance

✳ A *conviction* that gives a reasonable explanation for why numbers 1 and 2 are so different—a belief system, worldview, philosophy, or religion[13]

To this list I would also add:

* A *communication system* that helps them become more transparent and open to understand their loved ones and associates: words and actions that transmit a blessing to others.

* A *common goal* that binds like-hearted men together: vision, business plan, and strategies that bring men together for experience, action, and growth.

* A *church* that is real and connected to their souls; pastors and congregations are needed that will see men in light of their passions, interests, problems, and concerns. Men need places where burdens are unloaded, hope provided, and grace given.

* A *Christian experience* where the fruit of the Spirit and joys of the faith can be felt through an understanding that these rewards are only found when men are willing to suffer with Christ through self-denial, obedience, testing, self-sacrifice, and surrender.

* A group of *partners* who will surround them with unconditional love and support; people who are willing to "watch their backs," tell them the truth in a loving way, and model Christ's love in a way that helps them feel protected and safe even when the walls of life come tumbling down around them.

* A *wife and family* who provide a supportive environment where men can become renewed and restored. Men thrive in an environment of love and mutual respect. In the end, one of the most cherished things any man can ever experience is knowing that his family respects him.

BUILDING A PLAN

Here are some practical steps you can take to build a blueprint for your men's ministry. Begin by asking yourself these important questions: What do you see as some of the common traits you have identified in men that might need to be analyzed before you consider a plan? How will these traits influence your design of a model or program? What are the chief issues that separate you from the men in your church? Properly assessing what interests, expectations, and concerns your men have is critical to leading them to building a successful ministry to men.

Once you have addressed those questions, consider these action items:

* Meet with your pastor and discuss his vision and concerns for ministry to men.

* Talk to other men in the church.

* Look at models within your community of successful men's programs.

* Collect local census data about the men within your community.

* Contact Men's Ministry Catalyst to see if we can provide you with additional information at www.mensministrycatalyst.org.

As you consider developing a dynamic and effective ministry to men, think about the critical components found in Exhibit 1-B.

BIBLE STUDY

Read Micah 6:6–8.

☐ Why is God not interested in sacrifices? When have you made sacrifices for God?

☐ Put each of the following into your own words, and give examples of how each is done and what it looks like:

Do justly

Love mercy

Walk humbly with God

BEFORE GETTING
STARTED

In the first part of September 2005, I was relaxing in a Canadian hunting lodge after harvesting a huge bison and a trophy elk with a bow. As I sipped on my soft drink and turned on the television, I was horrified as I witnessed the fallout from Hurricane Katrina. It so shocked me that I felt a sense of guilt and shame that I was enjoying one of the best and most relaxing trips of my life while millions of Americans were suffering through an unbelievable experience that would affect the rest of their lives.

Hurricane Katrina hit the Gulf Coast, affecting Florida, Alabama, Mississippi, Louisiana, and Texas. It was the costliest natural disaster, as well as one of the five deadliest hurricanes, in the history of the United States. Among recorded Atlantic hurricanes, it was the sixth-strongest overall. At least 1,833 people died in the hurricane and subsequent floods, and total property damage was estimated at $81 billion.[1]

Upon returning home, I continued to be haunted by the images of so many people in anguish and pain. The sorrow in my soul so gripped my emotions that within a week God moved my heart to put together a group of people to join me in a mission to the Gulf Coast to see how we could help the stricken victims. After gathering some clothing donations and cases of helpful resource materials, we took a flight to New Orleans. Our commercial airline flight was the first one to land in New Orleans International Airport since the hurricane. The airport had been closed due to the destruction and the fact that it was being used as a temporary mortuary. The stench of death and blood-soaked stains still manifested itself in the marble floor of the main terminal. The faces of the clean-up people projected fear, frustration, and a degree of hopelessness.

We gathered our bags and resource books, then headed to an orientation center. After receiving our shots, a map, and a borrowed van, we headed out to our first destination: ground zero. The devastation was overwhelming. Our team looked to me for direction as to how we would start, where we would go, what we would do. The burden of even trying to wrap my mind around these questions became a challenge in itself.

Where does one start? The reality is that you can't start serving and assisting others until you first assess the situation, pray about what you see and hear, develop a plan, deploy your resources, and ask the Holy Spirit to direct your path. In a disaster like Katrina, you start by lending assistance to one person or family at a time, cleaning up one house at a time, counseling one broken heart at a time, and praying for one person at a time. And that is what we did. After ten days in the area, we had delivered food and water to hundreds of families, provided helpful resource tools and Bibles to thousands, helped wash down some homes, and counseled many distressed individuals.

Ministering to men is not much different than viewing the chaotic scene found in New Orleans. Men have been affected by many factors that have distorted their values, self-worth, and

> The target for an intentional leader is to provide ministry to every man in the church regardless of age, interest, talent, and giftedness.

faith. Most churches have failed to connect, train, empower, and deploy men as Christ did with His original disciples. The women's liberation movement increased the chaos by urging women to take over many leadership positions within the church. Today there is a lack of biblical male role models for men to follow. Men tend to be loners and lack the comrades of healthy male friendships. Unfortunately too many men in the church today have become spectators leading undisciplined lives instead of being active participants in partnership with the Holy Spirit in studying and applying God's Word.

Men's ministry is not just a group of donut eaters who meet once a week at a restaurant for Bible study. Any male attending your church should be considered as a candidate for men's ministry. It matters not if they choose to serve with an established group of men who meet for retreats and breakfast programs, or if they serve by teaching Sunday school, or if they sing in the choir, or if they do service projects. The target for an intentional leader is to provide ministry to every man in the church regardless of age, interest, talent, and giftedness.

INTENTIONAL LEADER

What is an intentional leader? As witnessed throughout Scripture (Matt. 14:28–31; Luke 10:1; 22:7–13; John 6:5–6), Christ was an intentional leader. Jesus was purposeful in His relationships, and often involved Himself in the daily lives of others. He developed teams, created plans, directed His men, challenged others to address risks and faith, allowed people to fail; yet He was there to assist them, and He met people where they were. Christ's methods, teaching, and training were divinely guided to make the most out of His time with others. He helped motivate and move people along in their spiritual journeys.

If we are to be intentional leaders, we need to care enough to relate on a personal basis to those whom God puts in our path to disciple. This will require that we deliberately invest ourselves in the lives of others, taking time and effort to get to know them intimately, looking for ways we can strengthen them and challenge them, and spending time one-on-one or in groups teaching them from God's Word. But above all else, the intentional leader is also a man who deliberately practices what he preaches, who strives daily to live in obedience to the commands of Christ.

SPIRITUAL MENTOR

As God put upon my heart to write *The Spiritual Mentor*, several new concepts evolved about this subject. Previous books I've written on the subject utilized many of the modern-day concepts about how we go about discipling (mentoring) others. As I developed *The Spiritual Mentor* I was directed back to the words of Christ and how His disciples applied the principles to

> A spiritual mentor is a person who disciples another person through the use of relational platforms so as to fully connect with the person one is mentoring.

establishing the first-century church. It would be important in developing a thorough understanding of this subject to read the companion work to this project first.

In my mind, there is a biblical distinction between a person who simply mentors someone and a spiritual mentor or true discipler of others.[2] The Oxford English Dictionary defines a *mentor* as "an experienced and trusted advisor or guide; a teacher or tutor."[3] Secular mentors often use social areas such as work, hobbies, education, and sports as a way to build relationships with others. A mentor in a sense becomes a trusted adviser, counselor, teacher, and guide to someone. Typically, a mentor is a more mature person than the person being mentored.

I define a spiritual mentor as a person who disciples another person through the use of relational platforms[4] so as to fully connect with the person one is mentoring. Being a spiritual mentor is ultimately about building a relationship that can help both parties become stronger in their faith. If we agree that the most precious of gifts is *time*, then the idea of investing in others or having someone invest in you is a special thing.

God's Word tells us that every Christian is designed to be a disciple-maker for Jesus. It is the responsibility of every church to equip, motivate, and deploy its members to serving our Lord.

As Jesus was an intentional leader, so every pastor, elder, men's leader, dad, mom, small group leader, and friend of an unsaved person is also a person of influence. Thus, we all have the responsibility of being an intentional spiritual mentor. We lead by example, discipline, and seeking to apply the Word of God in our daily living. Intentional disciples buy into the process of developing disciples using Christ's modeling, and value a team approach (the church) to reaching others.

An intentional disciple knows the spirit and gifting of those he works with (Eph. 4:11–13). Some readers will say, "I'm not educated and trained as an intentional spiritual mentor." But spiritual mentors come from all walks of life. They are men who have an interest in seeing others come to Christ. Being intentional about our approach to the process will require preparation on our part.

We can't model what we don't know; hence, a good understanding of God's Word is important to our ability to be transparent, supportive, and real to those we meet. We strive to obtain a biblical worldview in order to teach others the same. Spiritual mentors are guided by the Holy Spirit to understand where a person is in his spiritual journey. Are the people whom God has put in your path dead to spiritual things, new in the faith, young in their understanding of God's Word, or seeking to dig deeper into knowing God and making Him known?

In the purest sense, discipling a person requires that you be focused upon the spiritual development of an individual. Discipling a person is helping that person become Christlike in his motives, attitudes, and daily living. Pat Morley gave a good working definition in his book *Pastoring Men*: "A disciple is someone called to live 'in' Christ, *equipped* to live 'like' Christ, and sent to live 'for' Christ."[5] Thus, a discipler is a person who will help equip the disciple to become more like Christ so he in turn can disciple others.

Mentoring and discipleship are very similar, and you will find in this chapter that I use the terms interchangeably; however, the essence of discipleship is finding a *spiritual mentor* with whom you can connect. The term *spiritual mentoring* implies the heart of discipling another person within the context of a relational mentoring environment. That is to say, the most effective and long-lasting discipling relationships happen best when you seek to encourage and equip the person in areas beyond just the spiritual aspects of life. If you can find common interest areas, such as sports, hobbies, cultural interests, work, or family, your relationship will have dimensions that will help hold you together during trying times. Discipling others is more than a slick program, intriguing activity, or trite slogan. Major life changes occur during teachable moments that aren't always planned.

During the time of Christ, a spiritual teacher or mentor was called *didaskalos* (Luke 2:46; Acts 5:34). Jewish teachers taught through the use of a discipleship process, allowing the students to ask questions to which the teacher would reply. They did not have any official position and received no salary. These mentors were common men who cared enough about others to share their lives and experiences to help others deal with life.[6]

OUR CULTURE

A flood of issues have distracted and discouraged men from knowing God and making Him known. The primary purpose of this book is to equip and motivate men about building dynamic men's ministries that project Christlike models of spiritual mentorship, but first we will explore some of the barriers that have created uncertainty in deploying men to know, love, and serve God.

Through the collective wisdom of our Men's Ministry Catalyst team and my experiences in New Orleans, God showed me a simple process to help direct our team on how we could serve. In the same way, an effective pastor or men's leader (intentional leader) will take the time to first *assess* the dynamics of his ministry to men, pray about what he sees and hears, develop a plan, deploy his resources, and ask the Holy Spirit to direct his path. My experience and research testifies that this initial step is often overlooked or disregarded by people in leadership. It is also the main reason why we see the ebb and flow of passions for men's ministry within a church.

ASSESSMENT

Let's consider what *assessment* looks like for the pastor or men's ministry leader. The first part of assessment is understanding your culture, your church, and especially the concerns and ideas that each man has for building or participating in a dynamic men's ministry.

Over several decades, our ministry has developed various assessment tools that help leaders properly analyze the dynamics of their specific group. I encourage you to utilize Exhibit 2-A as one of the tools to analyze your group. We can't begin to seek participation until we understand the men in our sphere of influence at a deeper level. What are their interests, passions, fears, hobbies, work experiences, spiritual gifting, and vision for developing a relational environment to grow a healthy men's ministry?

The *second assessment* area is to understand the cultural challenges that men face, and how the church can meet the greatest needs of men today. Most men would say that there is an emptiness in their lives. Many men surveyed suggest that they feel:

✱ Lonely

✱ Emotionally isolated

✱ Friendless

✱ Confused about how to define manhood

✱ Success driven

✱ Spiritually empty

✱ Lured by pornography

✱ Deceived

✱ Concerned over debt

✱ Anxious

✱ Distracted

✱ As though they do not have relevant answers

For an intentional leader, the issues of the culture provide unique opportunities to reach men. God has empowered the church to help ignite the passions and energies of men by addressing the spiritual and social problems of this age. To effectively minister to men, the church must build a vibrant men's ministry with the following steps:

✱ Properly assess and survey the needs and interest areas of their men.

✱ Develop specific strategies and plans that stimulate involvement and commitment.

✱ Provide discipleship training and teaching programs that help men grow in their faith and develop a biblical worldview.

✱ Create opportunities for men to identify and utilize their gifts and talents in their churches and communities.

✱ Reach out to younger generations in creative ways.

✱ Encourage men to minister together.

The *third assessment* area is knowing the type of intentional leader who sets the model for men and for effective men's ministry. Developing a team of men (men's council) requires the pastor to be very selective in who he picks to be involved on this committee. Exhibit 2-B is a good tool to utilize as a job description. If a man is to be successful as a leader, he must first get it right at home (1 Tim. 3:5). It is important that a council member has his wife's support before he commits the time to get involved. We have found that the Agreement Form in Exhibit 2-C has been a great way for the man to fully consider the requirements for leadership in ministry to men.

The key to any successful men's ministry program is the senior pastor or other strong leader. It is our experience that senior pastors tend to fall into three categories:

Connected Pastors: These pastors resonate and participate in activities that "manly men" see as important (e.g., golf, fishing, hunting, team sports, etc.). Connected pastors participate in functions and strongly support men's ministries from the pulpit and by participating with the men in various activities.

Busy Pastors: These pastors relate to "manly men," but pressing time constraints, limited staffing, budget limitations, or geography hinders them from spending quality time with their men. Many pastors serve small to mid-size churches and do not have adequate staff to serve their members, especially men. Also, many pastors in our culture today are bi-vocational. They are supportive, but limited in what they can do.

Disconnected Pastors: These pastors generally have a fear of men. Because of previous negative experiences with domineering men or lack of positive male role models, some pastors really prefer not to have an effective men's ministry. They fear that men might take over their functions or become too involved with the running of the church. Disconnected pastors don't support or promote men's programs and rarely provide opportunities for men to work together outside of a Sunday service. They prefer to surround themselves with female staff members who they think can be directed and controlled. Our experience suggests that as many as one-third of the pastors we have encountered fall into this mind-set.

Fortunately, there are ways to help and support each of these pastors. This is best accomplished by bringing in a men's ministry consultant who can work directly with the senior pastor and help him identify a pathway to fully connect with his men. A team of godly men can surround the pastor, as Aaron and Hur did for Moses (Ex. 17:12), and encourage him to keep in the fight for men's souls. Our leadership model can also help the men better appreciate and value their pastor. Prayer support and acts of kindness go a long way to assisting a reluctant pastor to become involved with men's ministry.

PRAYER

The most meaningful answers to our problems come from the Lord. We communicate with God through prayer. It seems that in today's evangelical culture we know how to entertain, we know how to program, we know how to provide a worship service, we know how to build great facilities—but too often we don't know how to pray.

It is interesting to note that the disciples were with Jesus for three years. They witnessed Him doing great miracles, speaking to thousands, and challenging His opponents. In the final analysis, though, the main desire of their hearts and their major request of Him was, "Lord, teach us to pray" (Luke 11:1). In asking for this, they expressed one of the most universal desires of the human heart. Sometimes religiosity is substituted for genuine fellowship with God Almighty. It's through prayer that we can feel God's warm breath on our hearts and intentions. It's during our prayer time that things get worked out and answers are found that have previously eluded us.

Prayer is an encouragement for the strong and an impetus for the weak. During the precious intimacy of prayer, we have a chance to allow God to move our will into His plan and purpose. We are basically asking God for the privilege to think His thoughts after Him. A surrendered heart is forged on the anvil of a good prayer life.

One must still the mind and heart to really communicate with God. Communication isn't just sending a message, but taking time to really listen to what God is telling us. The psalmist was right when he wrote, "Be still [cease striving], and know that I am God" (Ps. 46:10). A successful leader will find a way to surround himself with trusted prayer partners who can intercede for the church and its leadership. Prayer will become an important part of the church discipline and attitudes.

WORK OF THE HOLY SPIRIT

Contemporary Christianity sometimes misses the importance of the Holy Spirit. Like the early post-apostolic churches, some churches seem to downplay the key role that the Spirit can play in the movement of the body. The excesses of some more charismatic churches have caused many to throttle the power of the Holy Spirit in the life of the church and its members.

We tend to think that men will be intimidated by something mystical and uncontrollable. The reality is that many men desire to experience all aspects of the Trinity. This innate desire comes to the forefront when grown men go to a sports event and yell their heads off almost to the point of exhaustion. The ministry of the Holy Spirit can empower and move men to action. Men want to be challenged and Spirit-directed so that they can feel and release emotion that has a positive impact. We need intentional and gifted leaders to help men appropriate and deploy the gifts of the Spirit.

Even in the Old Testament, we see that God used His Spirit to equip men for service. In Exodus 31:1–5, we find some of the instructions that God gave Moses concerning the building of the tabernacle and its furnishings.

> Then the LORD spoke to Moses, saying: "See, I have called by
> name Bezalel the son of Uri, the son of Hur, of the tribe of
> Judah. And I have filled him with the Spirit of God, in wis-
> dom, in understanding, in knowledge, and in *all manner of*
> workmanship, to design artistic works, to work in gold, in sil-
> ver, in bronze, in cutting jewels for setting, in carving wood,
> and to work in *all manner of* workmanship. (emphasis added)

Today, we need to connect with men on how to be open to
the calling God has placed upon their lives. That calling and
equipping can come through the movement of the Spirit in the
lives of committed disciples willing to follow God's leading. Our
role as intentional leaders (spiritual mentors) is to help people
know their spiritual gifting so they can apply their energies in
the right direction and help eliminate false starts. Men don't
like failure and, when they are encouraged to operate outside
their area of gifting and experience, they become frustrated and
begin to back away from tasks. It should be the goal of an intentional leader to know his men.

AUTHENTIC INTENTIONAL LEADERS

In today's got-to-have-it-now, synthetic culture, we tend to see
many of our products, promotions, programs, and even churches
adopt the "feel good" approach to resolving some very complex
issues. Too many faith-based ministries and programs have
leaders who are not transparent and real with their audiences.
While most men leading ministries are hard-working, dedicated,
underappreciated servants of God, some leaders tend to put on a
facade about their faith and lives. They cover their pain, temptations, fears, and frustrations by often distancing themselves from

their men. They know that men have a way of seeing through the fog of insincerity and recognizing the fault lines within their personalities, attitudes, and actions. It is critical that a good intentional leader strive to be real with his men. Those who can be trusted with a leader's confidence need to support, encourage, and protect their man from those who would attack him.

An intentional leader is comfortable enough to use his life—both successes and failures—as anecdotes to help his followers see his heart and how he handles challenges. In presenting my messages, I've found that the more I share my brokenness, hurts, pain, and sorrows, the more I connect with the audience. Men need to know they aren't alone in their struggles. Statistics indicate that 50 percent of pastors have visited a pornography site during the past week,[7] and this fact brings home the struggles that some guys have with this issue. And for those of us who won't visit one of these sites, we need to pass along our knowledge and personal practices that keep us strong when the storms of temptation flood the lobby of our minds.

The ways in which leaders deal with conflict and challenges help onlookers see biblical options to problem solving. This is probably one of the toughest areas for most of us. When someone pushes the hot buttons of our lives, we tend to react in the flesh. We often will distort the problem and over-personalize the matter, pretend that the problem doesn't exist, or direct ourselves to pleasing others instead of pleasing God.

A well-known pastor friend of mine told me a story about a time when he was a young preacher in the South. The pastor had been frustrated over a conflict with his board and found himself spinning in circles trying to please everyone. Finally, he decided to get with God on the matter. He pulled aside from

> All too often we seek to please man instead of thinking about how God would handle the situation.

the conflict and began to read his Bible and pray. Soon God gave him the answer: "For do I now persuade men, or God? Or do I seek to please men? For if I still pleased men, I would not be a bondservant of Christ" (Gal. 1:10). All too often we seek to please man instead of thinking about how God would handle the situation. Seeking to please God doesn't always resolve the problems in a favorable way, as measured by our worldly standards, but you will know that the heart of God was present and valued from an eternal perspective.

The key is to get started by asking God to guide you and your men on a mission that will affect the guys involved, as well as their families, businesses, and community. Much like our team's work in New Orleans, your men need to see that by involving themselves in the work of the church they can make a difference in their own lives, as well as the lives of others.

BLUEPRINT FOR SUCCESS

There is much more to men's ministry than developing a simple Bible study, or breakfast program, or community project. It requires intentionality and purpose. To be most effective, you need to assess the issues involved with developing an impactful ministry. Men respond best when they know their involvement is not in vain and they feel comfortable with the leadership, vision, goals, and objectives. The main idea of ministering to men is creating a band of spiritual brothers who seek to unleash the potential within one another to glorify our Lord.

BUILDING A PLAN

The apostle Paul described what it means to be a disciple for life:

> I have been crucified with Christ; it is no longer I who live, but Christ lives in me; and the life which I now live in the flesh I live by faith in the Son of God, who loved me and gave Himself for me. I do not set aside the grace of God; for if righteousness comes through the law, then Christ died in vain. (Gal. 2:20–21)

We are to live our lives in fellowship with other believers such that Christ will be seen by others. To do this, we must set our minds and hearts on the things of God.

How can you better integrate the following into your ministry to men? Can you be intentional about providing encouragement and opportunities for men to explore the following?

* Guided and personal prayer

* Accountability partners

* Reviewing together godly literature, videos, and social media

* Worship and praise

* Reading and studying God's Word

* Opportunities for mediation (private breakaway times in the outdoors)

> We are to live our lives in fellowship with other believers such that Christ will be seen by others.

* Giving a guy a call at work to encourage him in his day

* Inviting a guy out for coffee, especially during times of celebration (e.g., birthday)

✳ Recreational moments together (golfing, fishing, hunting, sports events)

✳ Creating an environment that helps explore the inner man (e.g., *Iron John, Braveheart, Band of Brothers, Lord of the Rings, All Pro Dad, The Spiritual Mentor*)

Remember that many men are dealing with a number of distractions (work, finances, self-doubt, bad family situation, low self-esteem). What can your men's group do to help men see God's plan for their lives? How can they better pursue God's heart?

BIBLE STUDY

Read Nehemiah 4 and consider Nehemiah's leadership during a time of opposition.

What sort of opposition did Nehemiah face? What motivated Sanballat and others in their opposition?

What tactics did Sanballat, Tobiah, and friends use against the Jews?

What tactics did Nehemiah use in exercising leadership?

Why did Nehemiah take the threats of his enemies very seriously? What did he do to prepare a defense?

How did Nehemiah encourage his men verbally? How might Nehemiah's actions and decisions have further encouraged the men?

OVERCOMING THE
MINEFIELDS
OF MEN'S
MINISTRY

Corporal Jason Dunham was leading his squad of marines on a reconnaissance mission during the war in Iraq when an American convoy was ambushed a short distance away. Dunham immediately led his men toward the action in hopes of providing fire support to allow the convoy to escape—but unexpectedly, the enemy turned their attention away from the convoy and toward Dunham's rifle squad. Within moments, the men were forced to leave their vehicles and move to positions of cover.

Corporal Dunham, however, selected three of his men to follow him as he circled around the enemy, determined to provide assistance to the ambushed convoy. What they came upon was a line of Iraqi vehicles heading in the opposite direction. Without a thought for the greater numbers of the enemy, Dunham forced the vehicles to stop in an effort to confiscate their weapons.

An insurgent leaped from the front vehicle, and Corporal Dunham immediately wrestled him to the ground. While

Dunham's men gathered nearby to prevent another ambush, the insurgent drew out a hand grenade and pulled its pin.

"Grenade!" Dunham shouted at the top of his lungs, throwing himself deliberately atop his enemy's hand—the hand still holding the explosive. In the words of the Medal of Honor citation that was later awarded to his family, "Corporal Dunham covered the grenade with his helmet and body, bearing the brunt of the explosion and shielding his Marines from the blast. In an ultimate and selfless act of bravery in which he was mortally wounded, he saved the lives of at least two fellow Marines." And in so doing, Corporal Dunham demonstrated the true calling of any godly man.[1]

Like Corporal Dunham, intentional men's ministry pastors and leaders can start out on a mission only to find enemies or improvised explosive devices (IEDs) in the pathway to victory. If a ministry does not anticipate the possibility of encountering these problems, then its efforts could be derailed.

One of the goals associated with this project is to equip you for the various trials, problems, and conflicts a group could encounter in developing or relaunching a dynamic men's ministry program within your small group or church. The things that can disrupt your vision of developing such a program may come from places you have not previously considered, and can be totally unexpected. As is too often the case, we ultimately see a men's leader throw himself on a grenade, sacrificing time with family, physical and mental well-being, and relationships with other males in order to try and save a floundering men's program. Sometimes this happens because of problems that come from within the ministry. If a leader failed to properly organize the program and establish a men's council (group of five to nine committee members) to help run the program, then he will probably become worn out in about fourteen months. Sometimes ministries fail because their vision did not connect with the pastor's plan for the church. Other failures from within occur when problems are ignored.

And there are times when the leadership fails to properly assess the cultural enemies attacking the church and its men's ministry mission from outside the walls of the church. Our culture is moving rapidly toward abandoning the Judeo/Christian values and principles that allowed us to express that we are "one nation under God." Why mention these cultural issues at all? It is appropriate to have a discussion on some of the issues that may derail your efforts in trying to develop a dynamic men's program. The reality is that there will be all kinds of outside interruptions and influences that will stifle your mission. An intentional leader will recognize those potential problems ahead of time and endeavor to educate, equip, and motivate his men to conquer the problems without losing men or ground in the battle for men's souls.

ASSESSING THE CULTURAL IEDS AND GRENADES

APATHY: THE FAILURE OF MAN

A growing myth in our culture is that men are hopeless and helpless. When surveying the social horizon and evaluating the many television sitcoms that portray men as stupid, inept, unorganized, lazy, insensitive, and sexually driven, is there any wonder why men are so disrespected within this culture? How did men get off track? Are guys to blame Gloria Steinman and the

Women's Liberation Movement of the 1970s for the distorted perception? Should men hold the liberal educational system responsible for having taken authority and honor away from parents? Maybe fault lies on the media industry with its debased music and games that encourage kids to devalue their parents—and especially their dads. Perhaps it's the belief that government will solve everything, including the lack of appropriate leadership in the home.

There is plenty of blame to go around, but the problem really started at the beginning of time. In Genesis we read, "Then God blessed them, and God said to them, 'Be fruitful and multiply; fill the earth and subdue it; have dominion over the fish of the sea, over the birds of the air, and over every living thing that moves on the earth'" (Gen. 1:28). God blessed relationships and delighted in the intimate fellowship He had with Adam and Eve. He knew it was not good for man to live alone, so He created woman. He also gave man the responsibility for woman and for her spiritual development (Eph. 5:25–27).

But man thought he had a better idea. The first failure of man came in Genesis 3:

> So when the woman saw that the tree was good for food, that it was pleasant to the eyes, and a tree desirable to make one wise, she took of its fruit and ate. She also gave to her husband with her, and he ate. Then the eyes of both of them were opened, and they knew that they were naked; and they sewed fig leaves together and made themselves coverings. (vv. 6–7)

Satan picked on the emotional sex to tempt her into breaking God's command. But where was Adam? By God's design he was

> Men must decide if they are going to be spectators or participants in the battle for truth.

supposed to have been the protector, the defender, the warrior standing up for truth. The reality was that Adam was standing by watching. Notice that verse 6 states that Adam was with Eve when she ate the forbidden fruit—implying that he was standing idly by while his wife was deceived by the devil! Evidently, only Eve actually talked with the serpent. Despite warnings from God, man stood and watched instead of getting involved.

How many men today are doing the same thing? Men tend to let their wives take care of problems instead of being the masters of their homes and the victors of the spiritual battles in front of them. Men must decide if they are going to be spectators or participants in the battle for truth. Are guys going to get their uniforms dirty by fighting in the game for the spiritual health of their family and nation? Preston Gillham put this kind of godly masculinity into perspective:

> "Masculine" is not something you do, and neither is being a Christian man a role you perform. Masculine is what you *are*. Christian *is who God makes you when you became a believer*. Therefore, being a Christian man is not a play you act out. It is living according to who God made you to be. Being a Christian man means living your life the same way Jesus Christ lived His. It is time to rethink our ideas. Masculinity has nothing to do with appearance, job, hobbies, accomplishments, family, Christian activity, or how many times you have been bitten by poisonous snakes. Masculine is who you are

and what you are. The challenge is not to *become* masculine. As Paul said in 1 Corinthians, it is time for us to "act like men [and] be strong."

Gary Smalley and John Trent say, "Men have always been hunters, warriors, and adventurers. The call of a challenge— whether it is picking up a sword to join the Crusades, setting sail in a small boat across the Atlantic, or tackling Mount Everest 'because it is there'—is something God has wired within a man."[2]

THE FEAR FACTOR

Another cultural factor that could derail men in their conquest to establish a dynamic men's ministry is that we tend to fear failure. Men do not want to see their work or lives as something less than important. Men, by their design, want to see themselves as achievers, contributors, warriors, and leaders.

COMMON FEARS MEN FACE TODAY

The fear of failure. Why would men get involved with something they are unfamiliar with—especially church? The theology, work, and politics of the church suggest risks that most men do not feel comfortable taking. Men want to feel they are prepared for the tasks at hand; so without proper training, coaching, and encouragement, most men will not step forward to help lead their church toward some vision or plan—if such a vision even exists.

One of the more subtle aspects of a fear of failure is that it is often mixed up with another fear: the fear of ridicule. A man becomes afraid to take risks simply because he is afraid that he will look ridiculous if he fails. Consider the apostle Peter, when he stepped out of the boat on the Sea of Galilee to walk on the water toward Jesus. Imagine how absurd he would have looked to the others in the boat if he had plunged straight to the bottom with his first step off the boat! And who ever heard of someone walking *on top of* water in the first place? Yet Peter overcame the fear of looking ridiculous the moment he stepped over the side of that boat—and that step led him to real spiritual growth. The risk of failure is the foundation stone for learning and growth. Here is the principle involved: Failure does not shape you; the way you *respond* to failure shapes you.[3]

The fear of transparency. No man likes to be rejected for showing his emotions or vulnerability. Most men have heard the words, "Big boys don't cry," or "Stand up and be a man!" The reality is that most men have the need to vent and show appropriate emotion at appropriate times. The church needs to provide the safe atmosphere that encourages men to get in touch with their feelings.

> Failure does not shape you; the way you *respond* to failure shapes you.
>
> **—John Ortberg**

The fear of appearing needy. When the *Titanic* hit the iceberg and began sinking, the message that repeatedly sounded over the loudspeakers was, "Women and children first." Many pastors believe that men should have a servant's heart and that, in most social settings, women and children should be first; but Christ modeled the principle that, when it comes to matters of faith, men should be first—that is, God has called men to lead the way. Men should lead the way, and then be sacrificial in their leadership and be servants—i.e., make sure that everyone else is safe prior to them moving to safe ground. Jesus' focus and mission was on discipling men—specifically, twelve men who would become the leaders of their homes and communities. Pastors need to convey to men that they are indispensible in fulfilling the mission of the church.

The fear of breaking some orthodoxy or liturgical rules. Most churches aren't into risk-taking. Generally, men like to work the edge of life. Risk is identified in much of what they do. They often choose their recreation and pastime activities based upon the risk and reward. Being a follower of Christ requires some risk—why else would Jesus have told His disciples to not fear before sending them out in Matthew 10? God's Word tells us 366 times not to fear. Pastors need to help men to "fear not" when it comes to serving the Lord.

The fear that there is not a comprehensive strategy and vision for men's ministry. Men follow men, not programs or religions. They can become fearful when basic organization, goals, and objectives are *not* in place. Men like to see that their efforts lead to successfully meeting the objectives. Guys appreciate knowing that their time has value to those they serve. Pastors who see their men engaged in the work of the church have found ways to effectively communicate their vision, plans, and goals to the men of the church. Successful pastors utilize a team approach to problem solving and vision planning. They promote the use of practical tools like the ones found in this project.

Developing a vision and mission for a dynamic and effective ministry to men is critical to its success. Without a plan, a vision, goals, and objectives, failure is just over the horizon. Thus, Exhibit 3 will help you develop some of the components for setting an initial course for your ministry.

The fear of loneliness and isolation. The tension of this modern culture has created much stress. Typically, when men are under stress, they flee from others and retreat to a lonely place where they can try to work things out. The typical church environment could be threatening to guys seeking space and a private place to contemplate decisions. Most women see church as a refuge and a place for fellowship, understanding, and support. Men need to work harder at providing opportunities for guys to be real with their struggles and failures. Specific small group sessions need to embrace those who are lonely and frightened about life. As churches begin to help men see the value of fellowship within a vibrant and caring men's ministry, it will see more men making their faith and church a priority.

SPIRITUAL WARFARE

The apostle Paul was no stranger to spiritual warfare. In writing to the Christians in Ephesus, he noted that "we do not wrestle against flesh and blood, but against principalities, against powers, against the rulers of the darkness of this age, against spiritual hosts of wickedness in the heavenly places" (Eph. 6:12). The temptations, footholds, and strongholds that men face in today's culture create enormous pressure for many Christians. Often there is a progression of sin in our lives if we do not turn away from the many temptations of this world.

A temptation is a trial or test. Whether it's putting inappropriate charges on an expense report, taking a glance at a pornographic website, cheating on taxes, or having a flirtatious relationship with a co-worker, we are putting our faith and patience to a test. The tempter, Satan (Matt. 4:3), is like a roaring lion soliciting our participation in things that erode our character and Christian testimony.

Paul warned the Christians in Ephesus, "do not give the devil a foothold" (Eph. 4:27 NIV). The Greek word translated "foothold" or "place" is *topos*, from which we get the word *topography*. It refers to a small location—not a whole nation or mountain range, but just a little spot, just big enough for a person's toe. Paul was warning his readers that the devil only needs a space big enough for his toe in order to work his way into a believer's life. Picture the devil as a rock climber on a steep, vertical cliff face. He does not have a nice staircase cut into the cliff to walk up; instead, he searches diligently for the tiniest cracks, the most insignificant little bumps of rock—and when he finds them, he jams his toes into the cracks and grips the bumps like iron.[4]

Once we succumb to temptation and allow Satan a foothold in our lives, the next step is for the sin to become an addiction or *stronghold*. A stronghold is a fortified place that so dominates our lives that our primary focus on Christ and building a godly character no longer becomes our passion. That is precisely why Paul encourages us: "Therefore take up the whole armor of God, that you may be able to withstand in the evil day, and having done all, to stand" (Eph. 6:13).

Jesus wants us to walk in the light of His Word and not be held hostage to the darkness of sin. Like Corporal Dunham, we must be prepared to meet the enemy where we find him. In John 21, Christ asked His disciples if they were willing to die for their convictions. Are you ready to die for the sake of Christ? Are you ready to die to self and your worldly lusts?

BLUEPRINT FOR SUCCESS

What cultural IEDs and enemies are keeping you from developing and deploying a vision of impacting your men for Christ? List the three major roadblocks you see that could prevent you from reaching your goal.

What are some of the things you could do to positively assert godly leadership into your marriage, workplace, and church?

Describe the vision and specific goals you see in developing a dynamic men's ministry outreach to the men of your group or church.

BUILDING A PLAN

Meet with intentional leaders of your small group or church and discuss the vision, plan, and goals and objectives for your ministry to men.

Through spiritual mentoring, groups identify intentional leaders who will take the time, energy, and resources to engage men on a one-on-one basis. When we show men that we are really interested in them at their workplace, home, and areas of interest, they will begin to connect with other men and the church. Bring a lunch to someone at their workplace and share some time with them as you learn what they do and who they know, and discover how they can be actively involved in a vibrant and life-changing men's ministry.

BIBLE STUDY

☐ What are the cultural values of today that influence you and your family the most? Which ones are most influential among your friends? Are you storing up treasures here on earth, or treasure in the kingdom of heaven (Matt. 6:19–21)?

☐ How would these verses of Scripture influence your vision for ministry to men (Prov. 15:22; 16:1, 3; 19:21; 21:5; 29:18)?

☐ Read Psalm 27. This psalm is virtually brimming with spiritual gems. To summarize David's eloquent expressions, we can sift the following truths that can be used to fight off attacks of fear:

> *Seek God's protection:* "Safety sits with me in the hiding place of God. He will set me on a rock, high *above the fray*" (v. 5 The Voice).
>
> *Worship God's majesty:* "I will sing praises to the LORD" (v. 6).
>
> *Pray:* "hear my cry and respond with Your grace" (v. 7 The Voice).
>
> *Focus on the Lord:* "I am seeking You" (v. 8 The Voice).
>
> *Study God's Word:* "Teach me Your way, O LORD, and lead me in a smooth path" (v. 11).
>
> *Be confident:* "I am still confident of this: I will see the goodness of the LORD in the land of the living" (v. 13 NIV).
>
> *Be patient:* "Wait for the Eternal" (v. 14 The Voice).
>
> *Be courageous:* "Be of good courage" (v. 14).

This is what you and I must do. Fear not—He is with you always. The Lord is the stronghold of your life!

☐ What are three fears that try to rob you of a joyful life?

☐ How is God bigger than your fears?

☐ Read God's comforting Word to help you overcome your fears (Pss. 27:2; 91:1; Isa. 51:12–16; Rom. 8:15; 2 Tim. 1:7; 1 John 4:18).

☐ What do the following scriptures say about spiritual warfare?

James 4:1–4
1 Peter 4:1–4
1 Peter 5:8
Ephesians 6:12

DEVELOPING
THE TEAM

Michiko Kakutani published a well-documented article in the *New York Times* on May 8, 2011, detailing some of the qualities given to the training and intensity involved in becoming a Navy SEALs commando. "They [the SEALs] are America's Jedi knights: the elite of the elite, an all-star team of commandoes, 'tier one' special operations warriors given mission-impossible assignments in the most dangerous parts of the planet."[1]

Certainly this describes the type of individuals involved in the raid on Bin Laden's headquarters, when the number one terrorist was taken out and important intelligence information was discovered. This mission reminded Americans that we have many young men and women who daily stand watch and are willing to sacrifice their lives so that we might enjoy the benefits of living in a free country. "Members of [SEAL] Team 6 have reportedly hunted down war criminals in Bosnia, engaged in some of the fiercest battles in Afghanistan, and in 2009 they took down three Somali pirates and rescued an American hostage with just three bullets."[2]

Beyond their intense training, high-tech equipment, and ability to manage fear is the unique bond that is created from building a strong team. When it is all on the line, these valiant warriors must trust and depend upon the other members of the team. Because their work is very sensitive, they work anonymously and without public recognition, often leaving family members in the dark for months without any communication.

SEAL squads are normally divided into six- to eight-men teams of well-conditioned, athletic soldiers who are cross-trained in a number of duties. A platoon typically has sixteen operators. Among the skill sets you might find within a SEAL platoon are Sniper, Breacher, Communicator, Maritime/Engineering, Close Air Support, Corpsman, Point-man/Navigator, Primary Driver/Navigator (Rural/Urban/Protective Security), Heavy Weapons Operator, Sensitive Site Exploitation, Air Operations Master, Lead Climber, Lead Diver/Navigator, Interrogator, Explosive Ordnance Disposal, Technical Surveillance, and Advanced Special Operations. More important than individual recognition, personality quirks, philosophical differences, and racial barriers is the mission of the team. Like developing a beautiful mosaic, each team member has a place and a purpose. When assembled correctly, the mosaic takes form and becomes more significant than any single piece.

BUILD A TEAM

The typical men's ministry program consists of one guy who, with the help of a few buddies, develops an idea on what might be of interest to others within the group. It usually takes about fourteen to eighteen months before the leader implodes due to the pressures of trying to go it alone. The pastor then looks for another willing soul and challenges him to the same tasks. What

Most men's ministries experience
the ebb and flow of some success
accompanied by many failures;
and thus, significant momentum
in men's ministry is never realized.

usually happens is that most men's ministries experience the ebb
and flow of some success accompanied by many failures; and
thus, significant momentum in men's ministry is never realized.

Ministry to men works best when a group of three to eight
men with various backgrounds and skill sets come together
to work as a team. The mission of the team is based upon the
vision statement and goals that are specific to the men within
the church. And yes, they must overcome and learn how to
handle fear. The fear of failure haunts many potential leaders.
Men see themselves as incompetent or weak if they fail. This
myth prevents too many guys from trying innovative ideas and
developing dynamic men's ministries because they worry about
failing. In part, that is why this book was developed: to help
eliminate 90 percent of the common failure points that leaders
worry about when developing ministry to men.

Our experience has demonstrated that, when a pastor estab-
lishes a team and empowers them to a cause with a clear purpose,
men will respond and people will get involved. King Solomon
wrote, "In the same way that iron sharpens iron, a person sharpens the character of his friend" (Prov. 27:17 The Voice). Solomon
was thinking of a team. We need one another for accountability,
encouragement, enlightenment, and fellowship. Team is at the

very essence of our Christian faith. The very character of God, the triune Godhead, provides for us a healthy leadership team model that we can replicate throughout the church's various ministries.

TEN STEPS TO DEVELOPING A TEAM CULTURE

1. RALLY YOUR MEN

Before any successful military engagement, the warriors are rallied with a call to arms. Usually the highest-ranking person in the group will bring the men together so he can discuss the vision and plan while encouraging men to fight the good fight.

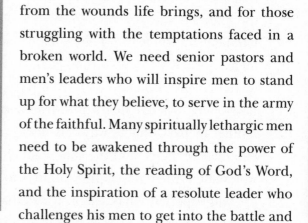

Ministry to men works best when a group of three to eight men with various backgrounds and skill sets come together to work as a team.

The reality is this: Christian men are in a battle for lost souls, for those who are in pain from the wounds life brings, and for those struggling with the temptations faced in a broken world. We need senior pastors and men's leaders who will inspire men to stand up for what they believe, to serve in the army of the faithful. Many spiritually lethargic men need to be awakened through the power of the Holy Spirit, the reading of God's Word, and the inspiration of a resolute leader who challenges his men to get into the battle and win the fight. Spiritual battles aren't won by those who watch from the sidelines, but by men who are in the trenches, who advance forward, and who have a vision for winning.

2. CREATE A "WE CULTURE"

SEAL Team 6 was successful in executing its mission on Bin Laden because hundreds of dedicated men and women provided intelligence, surveillance, security, specialized equipment, and protection for the team on the ground. The team recognized that their efforts would not have been successful without the spotters on the ground, the jet fighters who threatened the Pakistani planes and helicopters, the refueling stations, and the direction from mission control. The people associated with this mission developed a "we culture." No one branch of the military service can take credit for the successful mission.

In a similar manner, if the senior pastor builds an environment where the men's ministry leaders (and, for that matter, the entire church) think in terms of "we," everyone will feel supported and part of the team. I have seen churches that utilize this concept, and they have been blessed to have an amazing ministry to men as a result. Oftentimes, the "we culture" concept pulls men into the mission who normally would not be involved with the team because of their introverted personalities or spectator involvement with the church. People need one another, derive identity from one another, and benefit from working together. Teamwork isn't a luxury; it's a necessity!

A big part of the "we" is knowing that God must be involved. Scripture reminds us that prayer and God's guidance are needed to be successful in whatever we do: "Unless the LORD builds the house, they labor in vain who build it; Unless the LORD guards the city, the watchman stays awake in vain" (Ps. 127:1).

3. CLEARLY DEFINE THE MISSION

Those individuals from many different agencies provided SEAL Team 6 with the details on how to implement the mission. They formulated a plan of attack on how the mission would be handled, including contingency plans for the surprises that might occur. The team was prepared for those locals who rallied their forces to confront the intruders. There were satellites that relayed in real-time specifics that would help the commanders make good decisions on the ground and in the operational headquarters.

> Leaders who want to direct men need to formulate a plan that can resonate with the men.

Leaders who want to direct men need to formulate a plan that can resonate with the men. It needs to include elements of risk, reward, and adventure. Christian men are also encouraged when they can see that their gifts, talents, and resources can be utilized to achieve success.

An example of a plan that has these components could be a mission to assist single-parent mothers in repairing their homes or doing some yard maintenance. One of the churches we have worked with annually has a couple of Saturdays each year when the men gather for a nice breakfast and a short devotional, and then begin to attack a list of chores that have been screened by someone in the church. This is in addition to their monthly gatherings. In some cases, planning is necessary to purchase materials (such as lumber, paint, sandpaper, wallpaper, or herbicides) that can be used on a specific project.

The men should be armed with the specific goals and objectives of each project so they can recognize and evaluate when the mission is accomplished and what the spiritual "takeaways" are for each assignment.

4. HELP EDUCATE, TRAIN, AND EQUIP

Men in battle are successful in their mission because they have been educated, trained, and equipped for the mission they have been assigned. As an example, after passing a very tough battery of entrance qualifications, the Navy SEAL must endure over thirty months of rigorous training and education before he can be deployed.

It is the rare man who digs deep into Scripture to find the hidden nuggets of truth that will transform his life. Often what makes it more palatable is when men come together in a small environment where they can identify an opportunity (such as a mission trip) that guides them toward an end-goal that will allow them to deploy what they have learned and been trained to accomplish. When men can hear the Word of God in a relational setting where practical ideas can be used in real-life experiences, they feel equipped to share and become involved.

5. BE A DECISION MAKER

Decision making in the military is based upon a chain of command and written procedures. But even within this institutional setting, individual initiative is encouraged. American fighter pilots who have fought against Russian-trained pilots say that they see a real distinction. The Russian-trained pilots are so steeped in procedure and following orders that they don't have the "out of the box" thinking that has allowed American pilots to rule the skies in every major conflict since World War II.

Often a volunteer men's ministry leader is pressed for time. In an effort to get things done, a leader will make a decision that seems right in the beginning but may not have the support of the men. Unilateral decisions are quick to make, but many times slow to implement, as followers are reluctant to buy into the decisions. Decisions derived from team participation and consensus take longer to make, but they are backed up by greater cooperation and commitment.

Brainstorming with a small group of guys who represent various social, economic, and age groups will usually allow more "buy-in" to the concepts when presented to the entire group. We live in a society that most often sees decision making as a win-or-lose proposition. It need not be that way. Look for ways to create a win-win scenario where decisions represent the ideas of the various men in your group.

> When men can hear the Word of God in a relational setting where practical ideas can be used in real-life experiences, they feel equipped to share and become involved.

Let's say that many of the leaders are over fifty years of age and really enjoy more passive activities during the recreation time at a men's retreat. The younger men see the retreats as boring because there is no energy of things they like to do. The older guys may not enjoy running through the woods shooting one another with paintball guns but would appreciate an opportunity to have the young guys explain the operation of the guns and do some target practice on a defined range. This could be turned into a contest where age-integrated teams are formed and challenges are entertained.

6. USE TRUTH AND GRACE TO DRAW PEOPLE TO THE TEAM

The difference between a SEAL Team and a band of guys equipped with the same weapons and technology is that the SEAL Team guys know when and how to strategically deliver force. They are trained to only apply the force necessary to defeat the enemy and attain the goal. As a team, they show restraint and compassion when seeking to win over their adversary before strength and power are applied.

Today there seem to be a number of pastors who identify with the role of being a teacher-equipper rather than a shepherd-pastor of their flock. I've experienced the same traits in leaders of ministry to men. Jesus drew people to Himself and His theology through grace, truth, sacrifice, and servanthood. His compassion and warmth drew people to Him.

Christ's work with His disciples testifies to His commitment to building a team. While He preached and equipped them for service, He also prepared their hearts through examples of compassion and sacrifice and service. His self-giving love and kindness demonstrated that a strong leader can also be tender-hearted and forgiving.

7. GIVE MEN A GOD-SIZED MISSION

When President John Kennedy developed the concept of a SEAL Team, it was with the notion that they would tackle missions that were beyond the scope of most military units in the world. He wanted them to be the best trained and equipped and most honorable men the military could find. When the SEALs are involved, you know it's no ordinary mission.

And so it is with building a team of leaders to direct the affairs of ministry to men. Guys will respond to a pastor or men's ministry leader when the goal is a God-sized goal. As important as it is to have maintenance days at the church, many guys will not feel challenged with that mission. Instead, what if you rallied the men to go into the community and build a park on a piece of city-loaned land in an impoverished neighborhood? How would permission be granted? Where would the funds come from? How could the park be designed and maintained by local citizens so that they felt empowered? What opportunities would there be to witness to the community?

Most men want to be involved in things that can make a real difference. Develop big dreams and challenge the men to get involved. Teamwork is the by-product of a healthy, well-managed men's ministry where men work cooperatively toward achieving ministry goals. These productive environments enable teamwork to happen. I once heard a pastor say, "If you play a man's game, men come to play."

8. CREATE AN ENVIRONMENT WHERE RELATIONSHIP BUILDING IS THE PRIMARY OBJECTIVE

If a team in the military is to be successful in their mission, it's because they focus upon building trusting relationships. Can you imagine going into a hostile environment and not trusting the guys around you to cover your sides and back as you concentrate on the target? Each man on the team is assigned a position or sector that he is responsible for. If a guy fails to monitor his area of responsibility, he puts the mission and team at risk.

Within our church culture, we need to create the expectation that building trusting relationships must be of utmost importance. When guys need encouragement, someone from the team needs to provide that support. When a person shares his pain or makes himself vulnerable during a men's breakfast meeting, his story needs to stay with those he trusted in that conversation.

Relationships are forged over the anvil of intentionality. When men seek to really know and care for another brother in the Lord, friendships are built. To be intentional means that we take time to listen, observe, and interact. Good team leaders will build in opportunities for men to communicate beyond the surface stuff. An example might be the table questions given to the men after they heard a speaker at their men's retreat or breakfast.

9. HAVE A CODE

Navy SEALs are known for their teamwork and loyalty. But SEAL teams are founded upon some basic character traits that are fundamental to their success: a mutual trust and care for one another. To this basic formula they add another very important ingredient: good communication. Without these two important factors, a SEAL team would be dead in the water.

What can these benefits of teamwork look like when transferred to your ministry to men? They produce an unwavering trust and team spirit that give the team energy and a desire to push toward the goal. Mutual respect and brotherhood are created in captivating ideas, and creativity in accomplishing the team goals and objectives. By establishing better ways to communicate, men can solve problems. There is "buy-in" because people identify with the cause and are willing to take risk without being criticized. As we respect each person's talents, gifts, and personality, we can find ways to blend together our skills and abilities for kingdom purposes.[3]

Develop an efficient and fruitful business approach to providing ministry to men. Men respond best to good leadership and programs that are well organized. My experience indicates that men's leaders who attempt ministry with an organic approach (nothing really structured) usually fail. Most often men feel that following an organic leader is like following a ghost in a closet. Without becoming dictatorial or too bureaucratic, make it easy and fruitful for a guy to be involved with the Men's Council. Exhibit 4 will assist you in developing an efficient structure.

10. DEVELOP THREE CREWS FOR BUILDING A STRONG MINISTRY TO MEN

The Navy SEALs are effective because they understand the importance of individual gifting, interest, and training. They are a team of specialists with every man committed to the goal and to one another.

How can a group of volunteers in men's ministry develop the effectiveness of a SEAL Team? Our ministry has found that it is imperative to break down men's leadership into at least three separate ministry teams based upon their spiritual gifting and interest areas. (See Exhibit 4 for more details.) This is usually used once each man's gifts and interest areas are discovered through Exhibit 2-A. The teams are defined as follows.

1. Connection Crew: This team utilizes their abilities, networks, and interests in reaching out to others. The objective of this team is to connect men with the ministry of the church and to engage about participating in men's ministry activities. The men who seem suited for this team are the ones who are the outgoing planners and organizers within the church. It is important that this team maintain good relationships with other ministries of the church. They oversee the connection of the men to one another and the men's ministry growth and service opportunities. There is a special focus on drawing in unconnected or new men into the fellowship and making them feel welcomed and accepted, needed and appreciated.

This team is also responsible for publicizing and advertising all of the men's events (website, church publications, invitations, phone calls, signs, etc.). Often these guys serve as greeters and hosts at all men's events (breakfast table captains, retreat leaders, Bible study leaders, etc.). Because they are familiar with the men, these guys make good prayer partners.

> Develop a team approach to doing ministry to men.

2. Discipleship Crew: The objective of this team is to challenge, encourage, and equip men to serve others. These men develop and deploy disciple-making strategies to share with other men. Using Bible studies, small gatherings, and focus groups, men address issues that bring them closer to God, help develop them into better husbands and fathers, and help provide biblical solutions to life's challenges.

3. Community Outreach Crew: This crew focuses upon how the men can love Him and love others. The outreach team creates multiple opportunities for men to reach out to others. The goal is to encourage men to think about evangelism through practical acts of service.

BLUEPRINT FOR SUCCESS

The wisdom, insight, and vision that will build and maintain a successful men's ministry comes primarily from the Word of God, godly counsel, prayer, and purpose-filled discussion. Bible study for men cannot be a passive event. It must be active and involve men and give them practical applications for life and ministry. Men are goal-oriented, and there needs to be a specific, applicable lesson for each study. There needs to be something the men can accomplish, with results they can see almost immediately, because men need to see the results of their labor. They need to say to others, "My team and I did that."

BUILDING A PLAN

In Luke 14:25–33, Jesus shared the importance of counting the cost, which is also vital when appealing for men to be involved and make a difference in all arenas of their lives. When a presentation is made to men about getting involved in a project, it is vital to lay out details as to time, money, and talents that will be required. The plan also must include a start and end date, the amount they will be asked to give, and other important details.

A plan must also include a challenge. Men, because of the way God designed them, love to accept a challenge and then decide how to go about meeting that challenge. And they need a coach—someone to lead the way—a general, a captain, someone "on fire," motivated, and excited about the upcoming project. All of this is designed to connect with the various gifts and talents the men have and how they can best utilize them to get the

66

job done. Of course, they also need to be reminded in subtle ways that God Himself is pleased with the effort and the result.

BIBLE STUDY

Read Nehemiah 2.

What steps did Nehemiah take to prepare for the project of rebuilding the walls of Jerusalem? Why did he take these steps before putting together a team?

What did Nehemiah do to gather a team for the work of rebuilding? Why did the officials and others join his project so willingly? What role does the Holy Spirit play in this process?

DEALING
WITH THE
SINKHOLES
OF LIFE

On February 28, 2013, another of Florida's infamous sinkholes opened up, claiming the life of a man who was sleeping in his bed in the town of Seffner. Sinkholes often occur during times of drought when underground streams drain away or recede. Without notice an area can simply cave in, leaving people skeptical that even the ground they walk on and trust is capable of collapsing. The Seffner sinkhole swallowed Jeff Bush, leaving various other items in the room as they were before the hole opened and swallowed him. The hole took part of his bedroom and another room, without touching anything else. Because of the depth of the hole and potential danger to rescuers, there was no safe way to retrieve Jeff's body from the cavern.

For days after Jeff's death, friends and family knelt and prayed at the mailbox in front of the home. A demolition crew was called in to take down the house and fill in the large hole with gravel. The operator of the heavy equipment worked gingerly, scooping from the home cherished family belongings and gently placing them on the lawn. The demolition stopped on Sunday long enough for family members to pick out a few treasured possessions, including a family Bible. It was reported that one person, tears streaming down her face, hugged the Bible and said, "It means that God is still in control, and He knew we needed this for closure."[1]

> There are hundreds of men whose lives are like one of Florida's sinkholes, hoping that a friend or church will help mentor and direct them to a loving God.

There are hundreds of men whose lives are like one of Florida's sinkholes, hoping that a friend or church will help mentor and direct them to a loving God who can assist them during their times of trial and collapse. The failure of our economy, the loss of jobs, the numbing fatigue of our hectic lives, and the disillusionment with unsuccessful relationships causes many to feel as though things they previously trusted in can no longer be counted on.

A man who has claimed a deep faith in the Lord for decades recently e-mailed me to say that he no longer has hope. Some of the things of the world he once counted as stable, important, and cherished have spun into a bottomless pit. As a very bright and talented businessman, he was previously able to find a way forward when difficult matters hit his doorstep. Today he feels frightened, defeated, and lonely as he contemplates the future.

Where is the church when men like this struggle? Where are his mentors and friends? Is it because it's difficult for men to open up and claim their feelings to the church or a friend? As I ponder my friend's dilemma and try to encourage him, I can't help but wonder where we have failed in our Christian culture to create such a deep sinkhole between our faith and that which was displayed by the first-century disciples. Has our "got to have it now" mentality claimed our patience and perseverance in pursuing the Almighty? Has the church lost its way in how it connects with men?

WHY MANY MEN ARE NOT INVOLVED WITH CHURCH

The maze of liturgical thinking and formal ceremonies is contrary to what most men need and want in a worship experience. In his book *Why Men Hate Going to Church*, David Murrow clearly identifies many of the reasons why the modern church has failed to connect with men: "Not all church services alienate men, but many do. I think three things contribute to intimidating men in church: they are paralyzed spiritually, feminized socially, and demoralized religiously. Why is it important to get dad into church? Remember, 93 percent of the time, when dad goes to church, the family will follow."[2]

Also, various pastors have stated that churchgoers are more likely to be married, be good employees and citizens, and express a higher level of satisfaction with life. It is my considered opinion that church involvement is the most important predictor of marital stability and happiness. It helps move people out of spiritual poverty. Having a vibrant faith is also correlated with less depression, more self-esteem, and greater family and marital happiness. Religious participation leads men to become more engaged husbands and fathers. Teens with religious fathers are more likely to say that they enjoy spending time with their dads and that they admire them.

Exhibit 5 helps us understand where men are today and why they need the fellowship that can come from a good ministry to men.

THE ANSWER:
THE DISCIPLE-MAKING CHURCH

Is your church a disciple-making, spiritual-mentoring church? Are there opportunities for every man to participate in a disciple-making experience? How can pastors expand their thinking on how to bring others into fellowship with the living God?

Scientists keep looking for a holy grail that unifies the cosmos—a "theory of everything." Pastors don't have to keep looking. There is a unifying theory. Jesus taught us the Holy Grail for unifying His church. It's making disciples. Discipleship is the core mission Jesus gave His bride. Making disciples is the irrefutable biblical mission of your church. Discipleship is the process by which men become civilized. The institutional church is God's appointed means—the "first responders"—to help men become disciples. However, the church (in general) has not been making disciples at a proper pace. According to one survey, only 16 percent of church-attending adults are involved in organized discipleship classes, and twice as many women as men.

Growing men. More workers. Better leaders. Bigger budgets. Restored marriages. Curious youth. A balanced workload. A strong reputation in the community. An increase in first-time visitors. There is spiritual satisfaction.[3]

> Jesus taught us the Holy Grail for unifying
> His church. It's making disciples.

Points to Remember:

* The similarities of men dwarf their differences.

* No man fails on purpose.

* Men are tired.

* Men often have a lingering feeling that something isn't quite right about their lives.

* Men's lives are not turning out the way they had planned.

* A lot of men feel as though their lives are coming unglued.

* Most men feel like nobody really cares about them personally, with the possible exception of family.

* Many men are committed to a set of Christian values, but not to the person of Christ.

* Most men only know enough about God to be disappointed with Him. As a result, their lives feel futile.

* The feeling of futility is the chief tool by which the sovereign God draws men to Himself of their own free will.

* The sovereignty of God graciously and patiently orchestrates all the seemingly random circumstances in your life.

In my book *The Spiritual Mentor*, I go into detail about how to create spiritual mentors. We need a plan, an understanding of true discipleship, to help rescue our faith and re-purpose our men. The Spiritual Mentor must play a critical role in bringing the church back to its original purpose. We cannot forget that discipleship is a relational process that requires people to become actively involved in their faith. It is men who will lead their families back to faith. It is men who can help save the church from the challenges that other religions are placing on our culture. Devoted and active men are the ones who can passionately change the direction of our culture and its destructive patterns that are leading us into chaos and despair. And, most importantly, God has commanded men to be leaders in the home, church, and community.

WHY MEN GO TO CHURCH

The good news is that men desperately need what only a loving, nurturing, and Christ-centered church can offer. Through the ministry of the church, the following needs of a man can be met:

✱ To know God and really feel His unconditional love (Rom. 1:20)

✱ To find rest for his weary soul (Matt. 11:28–29)

✱ To fellowship with other men who are struggling with similar issues (2 Cor. 1:4)

✱ To hear God's Word proclaimed and related to in both practical and personal ways (Ps. 23:4)

✱ To feel inspired, encouraged, empowered, and understood (1 Thess. 4:18)

✱ To seek refuge from the world's problems (Ps. 46:1)

✳ To find ways to deal with the daily issues he faces (James 1:2)

✳ To find appropriate ways to model Christ's love to his family (Matt. 19:19)

✳ To receive moral and religious instruction (Ps. 32:8)

Once again, we connect with my good friend David Murrow's work *Why Men Hate Going to Church*:

> *The modern church is having trouble reaching men.* Women comprise more than 60 percent of the typical adult congregation on any given Sunday. At least one-fifth of married women regularly worship without their husbands. There are quite a few single women but hardly any single men in church today. . . .
>
> Tough, earthy, working guys rarely come to church. High achievers, alpha males, risk takers, and visionaries are in short supply. Fun-lovers and adventurers are also underrepresented in church. . . .
>
> Today's church does not mesmerize men; it repels them. Just 35 percent of the men in the United States say they attend church weekly. In Europe, male participation rates are much worse, in the neighborhood of 5 percent. This hardly sounds like a male-dominated, patriarchal institution to me. . . .
>
> Fortunately, pioneering churches and parachurch organizations are enjoying remarkable success in reaching men for Christ. New forms of worship and ministry tailored to the needs of men are springing up in the unlikeliest places. Some of the fastest-growing churches in America are also those most successful in reaching men.[4]

BLUEPRINT FOR SUCCESS

Scripture makes it clear that, before making any decision in life, one must count the cost, and, having counted the cost, one needs a blueprint, or a guide, or a plan in order to accomplish that goal or decision. The perfect blueprint for life and for abundant living is found in the Bible. Micah 6:8 states,

> He has told you, mortals, what is good *in His sight.*
>   What else does the Eternal ask of you
> But to live justly and to love kindness
>   and to walk with your True God in all humility? (The
>   Voice).

Physically, we are to "live justly"; emotionally, we are to "love kindness"; and spiritually, we are to "walk with your True God." Examine your life to see how you are doing in each of these crucial areas.

BUILDING A PLAN

During a small group meeting, ask the men to identify the types of concerns some men have. Make your question generic so that nobody feels on the spot to give a personal answer. Questions like: Can you identify the potential sinkholes in your life? What are the kind of things that suck you under? Discuss with the group how you can create a plan of identifying the potential sinkholes. How might you go about creating a list of people and resources that can help you cross over the sinkholes without being sucked into depth of failure and despair?

A good exercise to do with yourself and those you are working with is to make a list of three columns: physically, emotionally, spiritually. Then, under each column, write down both the good and the bad in that arena. How does your list measure up to what is required of each of us in Scripture? What do you need to change? What do you need to improve? What do you need to get rid of? Then, in prayer and reverence, ask God to help you in each area.

BIBLE STUDY

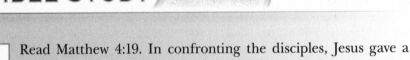

☐ Read Matthew 4:19. In confronting the disciples, Jesus gave a straightforward challenge to men. Where and how has Christ challenged you to follow Him? What holds you back?

☐ Read the gospel of Mark and record each instance in which Jesus made a difference in the lives of people. What effect did Jesus have in people's lives? How did He accomplish those effects?

THE
ASSESSMENT

Whether it is in business, sports, relationships, or ministry, a lack of planning will lead to failure. The wise counsel from King Solomon in Proverbs reminds us about the importance of good planning and preparation:

> Deceit darkens the hearts of those who plot evil,
> but advocates of peace have joy. (12:20 The Voice)

> Give Him the credit for everything you accomplish,
> and He will smooth out and straighten the road that lies
> ahead. (3:6 The Voice)

> Plans fall apart without proper advice;
> but with the right guidance, they come together nicely.
> (15:22 The Voice)

Luke 14:28 admonishes us in the same direction—to have a plan. Jesus said, "Just imagine that you want to build a tower. Wouldn't you first sit down and estimate the cost to be sure you have enough to finish what you start?" (The Voice). Probably the most important element to consider at this time is constant and consistent prayer. Proverbs 16:1 tells us, "People go about making their plans, but the Eternal has the final word" (The Voice). The pastor and his staff need to spend time asking for God's direction and support, and the pastor especially needs to be diligent in asking God for the vision He has for the church in regard to the men's ministry. Proverbs 16:3 commands us, "Whatever you do, do it as service to Him, and *He* will guarantee your success" (The Voice). And again, Proverbs 15:9 states, "The lifestyle of the wicked is repulsive to Him, while those who do right delight Him" (The Voice). The Scriptures are replete with admonitions concerning seeking the will of God.

It is amazing to me how often I meet successful pastors and businessmen who know how important planning is to the future of their organization; yet, when it comes to developing a comprehensive plan for their ministry to men, they fail to develop the design necessary to build a dynamic organization that can endure. Some time ago, I approached a pastor who was strategically located in a community whose men were primarily hard-working, blue-collar guys. They loved their hunting, fishing, and other outdoor adventure pursuits. The pastor was a very studious guy with good preaching skills, but he didn't really have a desire to connect with his men. For years, I took this pastor out to lunch to explore how we might help him develop a dynamic men's program. Unfortunately, it seemed the timing was always wrong.

After several men from his church attended one of our Iron Sharpens Iron Conferences,[1] they became fired up about ministry to men. They began to put pressure on the pastor, and he finally called me and asked for our help in putting together a ministry that would encompass all the men of the church. I suggested to the pastor that he personally request each man to fill out the church assessment survey our ministry developed to determine the interests and concerns that made his congregation unique. With some hesitation, the pastor encouraged his men to invest the time to go through the survey.

Some of the churches we have worked with have even set up a computer in the church lobby to expedite the process of filling out surveys. The collection of data from a group of men will help guide the pastor and his leaders on how to organize, plan, evaluate, and deploy men within the church.

The survey in Exhibit 6 can be customized for any church and sent electronically to each male member of the congregation. The results will be correlated and tabulated through Men's Ministry Catalyst (MMC) and returned with an analysis for the pastor and men's leadership team to review. One of the MMC teams will meet with the church to help decipher the results and to discuss a possible plan for activating and building a dynamic men's ministry program for your church.

THE LAUNCH OR RE-LAUNCH MEETING

The pastor and leadership team should meet to formulate a vision statement and a list of initial objectives, and to develop a six- to twelve-month calendar. These items should be based upon the input received from the survey. When men see a vision and plan that is passionately supported by the pastor with achievable objectives that involve fun, fellowship, outreach, and a chance to stretch their faith, an "all-in" mentality will be generated.

At a gathering of the men (breakfast or dinner), the pastor should present the guiding theology behind the vision and offer a powerful visual presentation that includes statistical elements. (A church involvement survey results form is available by contacting

Men's Ministry Catalyst.) A member of the Men's Ministry Catalyst team can attend this meeting to present information on the results of previous ministries and respond to questions the men might have. Most men respond best to presentations with a visual component that implies challenges, risk, and a God-sized vision. The objectives or programs should be identified using imagery, intrigue, and "can you imagine" thinking to help motivate the men to become participants, not just spectators.

There should be a blend of personal enrichment opportunities (men's retreat, Bible studies, small group meetings), outreach programs (big-screen sports contest, Saturday morning breakfasts, Outdoor Adventure Fairs, Back to the 50s event), and fellowship events that help men to connect with the guys of the church (affinity groups, SWAT teams, leadership groups, even an ongoing small group).

PERSONAL ENRICHMENT GROUPS

It is interesting to note that one reluctant pastor we spoke with prior to doing the survey thought that his men had little interest in personal growth. The guys who came to church were most interested in just showing up on Sunday morning for his sermons. After 70 percent of the men completed the survey, the pastor was shocked to see that more than sixty men wanted a Bible study and wished for a mentor. Neither existed in the church, and both were immediately offered to the members. Today over 150 guys attend a weekly Bible study.

One of the main purposes of ministry to men is for them to develop a personal discipline of studying God's Word and learning to apply it to being a more godly man, husband, and father.

> When a man sees that his gifts, talents, experience, knowledge, and effort has led to lives being changed, you have a potential critic turned into a contributor.

Encouragement and resources need to be spread liberally whenever possible to help men become passionate and accountable for knowing God and making Him known.

OUTREACH PROGRAMS

Nothing fires up a guy more than seeing that his participation and support of an outreach event resulted in seeing someone's life changed. Prior to such an event, it is crucial that your leadership team be equipped to "exalt Him as Lord in your heart. Always be ready to offer a defense, humbly and respectfully, when someone asks why you live in hope" (1 Peter 3:15 The Voice). An outreach event is generally directed to men who are not part of the church community. When a man sees that his gifts, talents, experience, knowledge, and effort has led to lives being changed, you have a potential critic turned into a contributor. Men need an excuse to invite others to church. Most unsaved men will not go to a traditional Sunday service or holiday program. If, however, there is something or someone that connects with his interest, then you have a pretty good chance of getting him to church. Some churches have opened their doors and invited the community to watch something like sports events shown on a big screen with popcorn and soft drinks provided. If your Men's Breakfast is more than a meal opportunity and you have an interesting topic or speaker, these events can be a good first-time exposure for the visiting participant. Programs that show guys having fun, being transparent, and exploring new ideas generally appeal to the unsaved.

FELLOWSHIP EVENTS

These programs are designed to help acquaint the men of your church with other guys. When guys participate in events like affinity groups (fishing, hunting, golfing, motorcycle riding, hiking, etc.) where men with similar interests or hobbies can spend quality time together, then guys tend to form bonds that lead to mentoring opportunities.

Hub groups are a form of affinity groups, but are more centered upon topics or subjects versus hobbies or outdoor interest. Hub groups often are born out of identifiable topical areas from the assessment survey, such as coping with addictive behaviors, pornography, discipleship, family issues, communication tools, overcoming depression, and other personal growth areas. The hub groups put people together who are working on the same challenges. It is recommended that these groups initially meet for four to six weeks. If bonds are formed and the group wants to explore the topic further, then they can continue.

Most churches doing hubs find that men respond best to meeting over a simple dinner, followed by an hour and a half to two hours of focusing on the topic, which should still allow them time at home with their families before the night is over. By promoting a variety of topics and speakers every four to six weeks, most of the interest areas where men are having trouble will be explored in a one- to two-year period. This allows men who have busy lives to enter and exit as time allows and their interests dictate.

The specific details and planning of the programs mentioned in this chapter can be found in the exhibits associated with program planning.

AWARENESS

Our experience has taught us that most men new to your men's program require being contacted personally at least three to four times before they will begin to seriously think about participating in an event. Research tells us that most churchgoing men attend church 1.4 times a month, which means in order to reach them at least three to four times before an event you need to promote it for three months. We will discuss in depth more about promotion and marketing in another chapter, because this item should usually come up in your assessment survey.

Many younger men will respond best when contacted through social media. Try to extend the conversation beyond a simple tweet or e-mail. Ask questions that demand a response. The same is true when approaching a guy in the lobby of the church. A typical conversation might go like this:

Leader: How is it going? My name is _____. What's yours?

Guest: My name is Sam.

Leader: I wonder if you heard about our upcoming outreach event called "Men's Night Out"?

Guest: No, I haven't.

Leader: Do you and your friends enjoy football?

Guest: We do.

Leader: Man, you have to invite them to come on Monday night! We will have our local college head coach there who will talk about football and faith. How about me calling you or sending you a text this week to remind you of the date?

Most men are very busy and also need a push to get them to commit. I have friends who won't commit to things until the last minute. Unfortunately, that is the nature of our culture. Do not assume that men will commit to attending just because your pastor announced it from the pulpit or it ran in the bulletin. You must have a team of guys working the lobby, e-mails, and phones. The invitation for men has to be personal, one-on-one, and often (at least three separate occasions).

WHERE ARE THE WORKERS?

When reviewing the two questions dealing with the interviewee's spiritual gifts, talents, and skills, make sure you identify your leaders and teachers right away. These are the guys who have the potential to organize and direct others.

One church we worked with felt that they didn't have enough leaders in the church to organize a program or help teach Bible classes. In fact, the pastor told me, "I only have ten men in our congregation who have volunteered to teach Sunday school, and you can't have them." I said, "No problem, just let me do the assessment survey and let's see what happens." It turned out that there were a dozen guys who had the gift of teaching and were willing to give some time to the church. There were another fourteen guys who were willing to take on a leadership role for specific events. All that was needed was someone asking them to get involved and then encouraging them along the way.

> One of the biggest failures of men's ministry is when the leadership team doesn't follow up with their men.

FOLLOW-UP

One of the biggest failures of men's ministry is when the leadership team doesn't follow up with their men. After the assessment survey has been analyzed and plans made, the pastor or leadership team needs to get back to the men, providing a report on a way forward. Just know up front that you won't please everyone with your initial choices. Explain to the men that your leadership team is passionate about doing everything with excellence; therefore, there will be opportunities in the future to review other options or to create an affinity group from the interest sheet.

An example might be that your church is in a metropolitan area, where golfing is more important than hunting. You have decided to put together an outreach event at a local golf range and bring in a Christian professional to help and head up your volunteer golf instructors. The six hunters in the church have long faces because they feel ignored. Why not hook these guys up so they can form the church hunting club? Give them the resources and tools to plan their outings so there is a spiritual dimension to their adventures. Make sure they have the support of an overseer (council member or pastor) so that the spiritual fruits of their efforts can be acknowledged.

THE MAIN THING

The main purpose of the assessment survey is to help men connect with one another so that intentional relationships are formed that lead to spiritual mentoring opportunities. Each and every event, program, and lesson ought to be directed to building a man's faith and creating opportunities for guys to develop deep and abiding relationships through transparency and risk-taking.

In this book and on our website, you will find resources to help you lead your men toward a greater understanding of God and His plan for mankind. Also, do not be discouraged if you have already tried to ignite your men but have failed. Try and try again. Develop a re-launch program that brings clearer focus on the vision and plan.

BLUEPRINT FOR SUCCESS

God's Word says that He has a plan for each of us. Unfortunately, when it comes to faith, too many men are content sitting on the sidelines (in the pews) instead of getting into the game (making disciples). When you can make ministry to men exciting, dynamic, challenging, and fun, you will be surprised what your men can do.

Here are five things our ministry has found that will ignite your men:

1. Create a vision and plan for your men to consider.

2. Passionately get your leadership team involved with the goal of connecting your men to the vision and plan.

3. Work on getting at least 80 percent of your men to complete the assessment tool; then report back to them as soon as possible.

4. Do not allow too much time between your survey and when you first engage your men with an event, hub, or Bible study.

5. Put spiritual mentoring at the top of your list.

BUILDING A PLAN

Follow-up is an essential aspect to assessment. Once a man gives you an opinion or suggestion, he wants to know that someone heard him. Even if his ideas are not implemented, he needs to know that someone cares enough to review his thoughts. From the assessment, the following needs to be part of your plan for getting the cooperation and involvement of your men:

1. Before and after the survey tool (assessment) has been given to your men, contact Men's Ministry Catalyst at www.mens-ministrycatalyst.org for guidance and counsel on developing and applying the survey. The sample survey on the exhibit can be customized to the specific demographics of your population.

2. The survey must be promoted from the pulpit, bulletin, and social media sites for at least three weeks, giving as many men as possible the opportunity to complete the form.

3. After receiving the results, the pastor and men's leadership team should meet and make determinations on a way forward for your ministry to men. This should be a multifaceted approach that includes various studies, events, programs, and opportunities for the guys to grow spiritually while becoming better acquainted with other men.

4. Your men's leadership team should contact potential leaders to move forward with specific elements of your new plan for ministry to men.

5. Within a month, report back to the men on the results of the assessment survey. Men's Ministry Catalyst can process the information electronically.

6. Do not attempt to do everything the first year. A dynamic ministry to men program takes about three years to develop. Pick out the top few elements and do them well.

7. Develop an annual calendar and stick with it. Your initial calendar should include the following opportunities:

A. One-on-one time for guys to develop the spiritual mentor relationship
B. Personal time for guided study and reflection
C. Corporate prayer within small groups when guys can be prayed for
D. Leadership development
E. Quarterly gatherings, like men's breakfast, men's dinner, or men's night out
F. At least two outreach programs, like Outdoor Adventure Fair, evening big screen movie, or a keynote speaker.

G. Annual Men's Retreat focused on developing and inspiring your men.

H. Quarterly opportunities to serve the community, single-parent moms, elderly, or disabled.

I. Small group studies on the Bible or selected topics.

J. Pastor appreciation event for your pastors and church leaders, such as a spaghetti feed, a movie night, or a simple outing.

BIBLE STUDY

Read 2 Chronicles 2.

☐ Why did Solomon ask King Hiram for a skilled craftsman to help build the temple, when he evidently already had skilled craftsmen in Jerusalem (v. 7)?

☐ Why was it important that Solomon know what he needed to build the temple, prior to starting the project? How does a leader gain an assessment of what resources he has and which ones he needs?

RELATIONAL
ENVIRONMENTS

At thirty-five years of age, I was reaching for the American dream of having fame, fortune, position, and power. I had moved forward in my career, and I became the youngest department head in a major park district. I was teaching part-time at a community college with aspirations of turning that into my full-time career. My success as a professional bass fisherman and record book archery hunter eventually led to Hall-of-Fame honors and a weekly television program.

I served on three boards of directors and was writing columns for various sports magazines. I had married the perfect wife and had twin sons who loved the Lord. How could life be more perfect?

Due to the pressure I placed upon myself and the desire to achieve, I began to have some heart issues. After visiting with three different cardiologists, it was determined that my heart issues were directly connected to my stress load—or so they thought. The reality was that my life was so out-of-balance that I couldn't sleep and had to resort to tranquilizers to help keep things under control.

My loving wife, Louise, decided it was time to go to a parenting conference. I thought, *This is going to be boring!* She had convinced our best friends Jerry and Jeanie to come along. They were planning on adopting a child so they were anxious to pick up all the gems of wisdom from the new guy on the conference scene: Dr. James Dobson.

On the way down to the Christian conference center, my friend Jerry asked me, "Jim, you have great kids; what is your secret to good parenting?" I sat up in my driver's seat and said, "Well, it's about providing quality time with the kids. In between my work, tournament fishing, teaching college, attending meetings, and going to church, I try and get the boys out now and then and make sure I tell them I'm proud of them."

Little did I know that Dr. Dobson would be speaking on the topic of what it takes to be a good parent. He stated that, to be a great parent, you need both *quality* and *quantity* time in raising a child. Needless to say, I felt like a mouse trying to creep out of a room filled with cats. Jerry, Jeanie, and my wife looked down the pew at me, as if to say, "Do you want to re-think your statement, oh wise one?" Dobson slammed me to the mat and that conference changed my life and the life of our family, eventually leading me to establish a national ministry.

During the next two years, I reconnected with my family and faith, quit fishing tournaments, got involved with the church, changed jobs, and basically endeavored to seek God's will and plan for my life. I decided it was more important to *do* what's important than trying to *be* important. My relationship with God and my family became vibrant. Shortly thereafter, several men I knew came to me for counsel and guidance on how to become a more committed man of God. They, like me, had been chasing the empty illusion of finding fulfillment in their jobs or hobbies.

About three years later, I noticed some hearing problems in my right ear. I assumed it was connected to my skeet shooting activities or the stressed life I had been living. After consulting with an ear, nose, and throat specialist and going through a special X-ray procedure, it was determined that I had a large non-malignant tumor that was pressing on my brain stem causing my heart and blood pressure to act up. Wow—what a shock!

As a healthy mid-thirties Christian guy, I couldn't understand how and why this would happen to me. After a month of failing various tests associated with my inner ear, I was scheduled for surgery. Before long, the day came for my appointment with the surgeons. As I left my den, I looked at all the management awards and tournament trophies and realized they would all be dust someday. These worldly treasures were empty relics that had no eternal significance. The only lasting rewards (family, ministry, friends, and God's Word) I could think about had eternity written all over them.

> I decided it was more important to *do* what's important than trying to *be* important.

My father came to pick me up to deliver me to the hospital. My wife and sons walked me out to my dad's car. I gave my boys a big hug and felt their warm tears against my cheeks. As we were driving to the hospital, I pondered the life I had led up to that point. I considered all my worldly achievements that fell short of really knowing God and making Him known.

That night, while I sat on the hospital bed reading my Bible, nurses periodically interrupted my meditation by taking my blood pressure, giving me shots, and hooking me up to all kinds of wires. As I lay upon the sterile white sheets and contemplated the pending surgery, I thought, *Is this all there is to life?* The doctors had told me there was a chance when the tumor was removed from the brain stem that my heart might stop and they would not be able to restart it.

After a nine-and-a-half-hour surgery and four hours in recovery, I awoke to a life that was different from the previous day. I had to learn to walk again as my balance was off, I had no hearing in my right ear, my right eye was not getting the tears it needed to keep it healthy, and I was experiencing some major depression. The doctor told me it could take up to two or three weeks before I could go home. I pushed the physical therapist to increase my therapy so I could be released sooner. Unfortunately, this led to creating a leak in my surgical site requiring another surgery taking three and a half hours.

> I looked at all the management awards and tournament trophies and realized they would all be dust someday.

After three weeks in the hospital, I was released to try and put life back together. My life would never be the same. As I settled in at work, the summer months came upon us. Louise and I attended a family summer conference where a young, unknown speaker named Chuck Swindoll was preaching. Chuck and I connected right away. He loved fishing and was a mentor in helping me process what I had been through and to focus upon some major future decisions.

I had felt called to ministry in high school, but went a different direction in becoming an administrator in business and for two public organizations. Little did I know that God was preparing me with experiences and relationships that would allow me to connect with men in a special way. He even used my background in fishing and hunting to reach people who might not otherwise consider the Master Fisherman—Jesus Christ.

When I told a mentor pastor friend of mine that I was thinking of leaving my job to attend seminary, he reminded me that I was in ministry already, reaching men through our Father/Child Fishing Conferences held all over the western United States. He told me, "Jim, you will reach men that most pastors will never see. Use your passions and interest areas to reach men for Jesus. Like Jesus said, 'Become a fisher of men.'"

My background and fame in the fishing world presented some unique opportunities to connect with others at Christian conference centers, churches, men's retreats, sports shows, and television where the gospel was proclaimed. It was amazing to me that God would take this East Oakland kid who loved the outdoors and develop a simple ministry to a place where our national board would be made up of well-known fishermen and business leaders like Jimmy Houston, Al Lindner, Homer Circle, Hank Parker, John Charvet, Jim Balkcom, and Joe Hall.

As God used our ministry to help direct men and their kids to Him, it occurred to me that men needed more than just verbal challenges. They needed practical resources that they would actually read and then put the concepts into practice. Many of my friends' wives would buy their husbands some of the books I was reading from authors like Bonhoeffer, Tozer, Barnhouse, Luther, and C. S. Lewis. Their wives placed books on the guys' night stands until the dust got thick, and then they would replace it with a new book. The men I associated with were not readers or theologians, nor did they have an interest in becoming one. They were hard-working, stressed-out guys who loved the outdoors, had dirt under their fingernails, and had a heart to serve others.

Why were these men not connected to the church? Why didn't our church have a dynamic outreach to men? Why were the number of men in our church declining? Why was it uncomfortable to bring my unsaved friends to church?

As I pondered the landscape of contemporary church and our culture, I noticed the scores of men who would periodically read their Bibles but felt they lacked the knowledge of how to practically apply God's Word in their lives. James, the half brother of Jesus, once said, "Put the word into action. If you think hearing is what matters most, you are going to find you have been deceived. If some fail to do what God requires, it's as if they forget the word as soon as they hear it. One minute they look in the mirror, and the next they forget who they are and what they look like" (James 1:22–24 The Voice).

First through story, then through articles, and finally by writing books from my experiences in the outdoors and as serving in the capacity of chaplain for two different NFL teams and a police department, I developed a style that I saw in the work of Christ. He used "orality" to connect men to faith issues. It is through stories and the practical loving application of God's Word that men begin a pathway to seeking deeper truths in His Word that transform them into the likeness of Christ. Pat Morley, founder of Man in the Mirror, and I have crafted a statement that bears repeating: "Give men what they *need* in the context of what they *want* (passions, interests) delivered in an *approach*

> "Give men what they *need* in the context of what they *want* delivered in an *approach* that produces *results* and you will have begun a process of *transforming men for a real reformation.*"

(relational environment) that produces *results* and you will have begun a process of *transforming men for a real reformation.*" Let's analyze this compound statement:

Give men what they need. Men need to feel respected, relevant, encouraged, challenged, and significant. Today's culture does everything it can to degrade men. Except for sports programs, almost every other television program portrays a man as stupid, hopeless, incapable, and spineless. Unfortunately, with the advent of the women's liberation movement and the withdrawing of male leadership in the home, too many young men are just coasting into oblivion as they incessantly play with their toys and game boxes, apps, and computers.

Today, more women are graduating from college than men. Women are beginning to dominate the upper management jobs. Even in the pastoral roles, we see more women being ordained than men in many denominations. Why is this so? What does it mean for our culture?

Before you send someone to protest on my front porch, please understand that I'm all for women having equal opportunities for success and competing in the workplace. The issue of our culture has as much or more to do with the failure of men than it does with dominating women. Tonight, over 41 percent of the children under eighteen years of age will sleep under a different roof than his or her biological father.[1] Too many men have abandoned their post and role of setting an example for their children. Consequently, children are growing up in environments where they lack a clear understanding of the proper gender differences and God's plan for the family.

There are some reading this book who have been impacted by divorce. And, in fact, "there go I but by the grace of God." Had I married the young woman I was going with prior to dating and marrying my bride of forty-eight years I, too, would be a statistic. We cannot change the past but with the grace of God we can impact the future. We can help young men seek a mate who will respect and support them. We can help men discover God's plan for their lives and encourage them to reach their goals. We can direct men toward God-size visions and dreams.

Are we intentional about creating a relational environment to help men establish goals, seek biblical solutions to life's problems, and discover their spiritual gifts and talents?

What they want. Men want someone to care and they want to be empowered to fulfill God's plan for their lives. They desire to be successful and to achieve those things that ultimately bring glory and honor to Him. They want to build a lasting and spirit-filled legacy that will stand the tests of time. They want respect from their mates and children.

Most men I encounter today do not have a deep abiding connection with another guy. The women in our lives seem to do well with establishing friendships that go beyond superficial things. They can quickly dig into feelings, hurts, praises, and concerns. Guys tend to be guarded and do not feel comfortable sharing many of our inner thoughts with others. Often the message we receive from our upbringing is "suck it up" or "be a man" or, in today's vernacular, "cowboy up!"

When we look at Christ, He was all man; yet He cried when Lazarus died (John 11:35) and again in Luke 19:41 when He wept over Jerusalem. Jesus felt strongly and with compassion over many things. Somehow we need to establish an environment where men can feel safe to express the deep feelings they have without fear of others judging them about their masculinity or avoiding exploring their own sensitivities in that area. We need transparent environments that promote conversation, trust, and healing.

> A relational environment provides opportunities for guys to safely explore their past and current challenges.

Developing relational environments that produce results. Relational environments are formed when mature Christians are willing to take the risk of becoming transparent. The most impactful preachers and men's leaders today are men who open their lives up and do not pretend they are perfect. They are guys who share about their failures as well as their successes, their pain as well as their accomplishments, their broken relationships as well as their homeruns, their temptations as well as their victories, and their mistakes as well as their positive attributes.

A relational environment provides opportunities for guys to safely explore their past and current challenges. We need protected places where attitudes, longings, temptations, weaknesses, and hopes can be explored. The leaders need to establish rapport and expectations that *confidentiality* is not negotiable. For guys, this happens best in a trusted mentoring relationship or in small groups. The expression "what's said here stays here" must be said prior to each time guys gather into relationship.

You build a relational environment by getting a few guys together to invest in developing an atmosphere and culture that promotes trust and security. These guys need to model what intentional relationships look like. By allowing two or three guys a platform to share how they built their relationship, we will testify to others that it's okay and healthy for men to have this type of relationship.

Even the configuration of a room and the way the lighting is set can help men become more transparent. Guys can connect with a place where they are known and accepted, and the more we do to make them feel comfortable and at home, the more quickly they will be willing to open themselves up.

In today's world, men are driven to succeed and many spend more time at their work than anywhere else, because the competition is so tough. They need a safe place to come to, a place where they are accepted and appreciated for who they are, and not so much for what they do. They seek a place where they can know one another on something other than a superficial level and be known in the same way—a place where a man can talk about the problems of work and home, and people understand and want to give help and godly counsel. It's a place where they can refuel to go back out to a pressure-filled and difficult world. It's intentional, it's comforting, it's strengthening, and it makes a difference. An intentional environment is a place not only where everyone recognizes you but also where some people can help you with your pain.

A relational environment needs to be modeled from the front by the leadership. How does that happen? Again, Exhibit 4 suggests some best practices for the Men's Council that will help form good relationships that can be utilized as a platform to work on the ministry as a team.

Transforming men for a real reformation. How do we change our culture? We can focus on government, but the reality is that government can't do an efficient job of creating a real reformation. Politics raises its ugly head and sides are chosen. Typically half the population will feel disenfranchised and not part of the solution. What about institutions? Schools, colleges, and universities all have their place, but by themselves can't change anything. What about our business community? Can they change our culture? Too many businesses are having difficulty keeping their own moral compass in the proper direction.

It's people like you and me who ultimately make changes, not politicians, institutions, or corporations with their computer networks or vast warehouses.

Can we expect children to make a difference? What about the highly educated and computer savvy younger generation? Children are great, and we do have some very gifted young people, but the reality is that we have pumped billions of dollars into our educational systems, youth programs, and faith-based groups to see the teen-related problems increase rather than decrease.

What about women? Did God call women to lead the family? No, He asked men to take that leadership role (Eph. 5:23). With so many absentee dads, passive males, and guys in pain, we need to encourage one another so that we can begin the process of spiritually healing and transforming people into the likeness of Christ, so that men are better equipped to be leaders in all areas of life.

In Romans 12:2, the apostle Paul helps us understand what transformation means: "Do not allow this world to mold you in its own image. Instead, be transformed *from the inside out* by renewing your mind. As a result, you will be able to discern what God wills and whatever God finds good, pleasing, and complete" (The Voice). We are encouraged to see an inward renewal of our mind, through which our inner spirit is changed into the likeness of Christ. Scripture tells us how to renew our minds: "Finally, brothers and sisters, fill your minds with *beauty and* truth. Meditate on whatever is honorable, whatever is right, whatever is pure, whatever is lovely, whatever is good, whatever is virtuous and praiseworthy" (Phil. 4:8 The Voice). We must be patient with ourselves and others as we see the continuous process of change occur within the context of an intimate relationship with the living God.

Through the study and memorization of God's Word, good preaching, close fellowship, and the power of the Holy Spirit, transformation can and does occur. When people are transformed and they group together as intentional leaders, then they can affect a real movement. Can you imagine meaningful changes with Christendom beginning at your church, within your community, and within your region that could serve as a model to impact our nation? It can happen, but it must start with you and me.

In the 1500s, great reformers like Martin Luther presented a clear message that transformed the lives of millions. Our world, and America specifically, needs spiritual reformers who have passion, vision, and a heart for those who are lost. We need a new direction, purpose, and plan to awaken people to the coming of the King.

It won't happen because we build great cathedrals or temples. Reformation isn't about developing slicker programs or more convenient ways for people to worship. It will happen because we build dynamic men who will help lead their families and friends to know God and make Him known.

BLUEPRINT FOR SUCCESS

This statement is worth repeating: "Give men what they *need* in the context of what they *want* (passions, interests) delivered in an *approach* (relational environment) that produces *results* and you will have begun a process of *transforming men for a real reformation.*" What do men in your congregation and community need? For sure, they *need* Christ. Additionally, they need companionship, comfort, support, encouragement, and a safe place to hang out.

They *want* to be respected, recognized, honored, and blessed. What approach is your church using to better connect with men, especially those who are broken and lost?

What would it look like to intentionally target the men in your community with God's message of hope and peace? You need to first build a dynamic caring ministry to men in your own church. What would that look like?

BUILDING A PLAN

* One of the main ways Jesus connected with people was through story. Build a testimony about your story. Don't be afraid to share your failures as well as your successes. Be

forthright in letting others know how God helped change your life.

* Think about three things that men need in your group of friends. What are the steps you can take to help men address those needs?

* What are the three things people in your community love to do (golfing, fishing, technology, etc.)?

* How can you create a relational environment so men will have the opportunity to meet other guys and eventually create bonds of friendship?

* Describe what might be part of your transformational process.

BIBLE STUDY

Read John 4:1–26.

Notice that Jesus was physically exhausted (v. 6), and had sat down for a rest.

Why did Jesus ask a stranger to give Him a drink? How might you have acted in a similar situation?

In what ways was Jesus going against culture by doing this? In what ways was His request very appropriate?

How did Jesus lead the conversation toward the gospel?

WE WERE
CREATED
TO BE
INTERGENERATIONAL

Recently I had the privilege of attending my granddaughter's graduation from a Christian high school located in the Southeast. Nothing thrills grandparents more than knowing that their children and grandchildren are walking with the Lord. "Grandchildren are the crowning glory *and ultimate delight* of old age, and parents are the pride of their children" (Prov. 17:6 The Voice).

It has been interesting to observe the emotions that our granddaughter Dana has experienced, as her high school transitioned from an older building into a new facility while she was in her junior year. The new building was a beautiful modern facility but void of personality and character. With the new building came a number of restrictions. The students were forbidden to put up posters or provide decorations or in any way "mess up" the sterile atmosphere created by the architect.

This particularly annoyed the upperclassmen, who had their own hallways (houses) in their old building. Of special significance was the senior corridor within the pillars of their former building. The seniors regularly gathered away from other classmates to discuss the things that were pertinent to their interest and future without the immature thoughts and acts of lowerclassmen.

The decision to integrate students so there would be no class distinction initially disturbed the seniors, and they looked for an answer—but the administrators had none. The seniors felt that their identity was lost, as they couldn't claim a territory like "The Senior Hallway" any longer.

After pondering the dilemma, a student suggested the idea of integrating the various classes within the new hallways. As the transition occurred, they began to see opportunities for the seniors to help mentor the lowerclassmen through the maze of confusion associated with maturing. As the senior leadership came together, they thought about the idea of naming the hallways after the founding fathers of their denomination and creating a unified and integrated competition among the four houses.

The idea caught on as the Christmas season approached, and the students realized that they needed to work together if they were going to beat the other three hallway groups as the Best Decorated House in School. Seniors began to encourage and work with freshmen. Upperclassmen ended up becoming role models and mentors to younger classmen, and the process started simply because some high school students wanted their senior year to count for something.

Let me illustrate this important principle with another story. Susie was a quiet and lonely girl who came to the Christian academy with the support of her single mom. Dad left the family years ago, and Susie felt abandoned and despondent. As

> When there is a blending of generations, everyone benefits.

is the case with most children who are products of divorce, she was trying to figure out what part she had caused in the matter. After getting her locker, she soon met a charming senior named Dana who had sensed Susie's despair. Within days, Dana began to approach Susie, asking probing questions like how she liked the school and what her family was like.

Dana felt compassion for his younger classmate and began to include Susie in a variety of activities. As they worked together on their part of the Christmas decorations for the hallway, Susie felt empowered and encouraged—so much so that she was no longer frightened about going to school and feeling like a failure, but she looked forward to meeting Dana and the other kids who became her friends.

BUILDING BRIDGES

It is often the case that, when we go to church or create a men's gathering, we come together by age groupings. The younger guys hang out with others their own age, and the senior adults are contained within their fellowships. Rarely do the groups come together to exchange ideas of how to collaborate about anything. This is one of the most unfortunate realities of the modern church.

Our ministry experience tells us that, when there is a blending of generations, everyone benefits. Just like the story of my granddaughter, fellowship and mentoring become by-products of intergenerational gatherings. When lives are shared, each generation can learn and prosper from the interaction. The younger men desire to learn from the failures and successes of wiser and older men. More mature men hope to be influencers and seek to better understand what drives younger men.

We know that Paul and Timothy had a deep mentoring relationship. In 1 Timothy 1:1–2, Paul wrote:

> Paul, an emissary of Jesus the Anointed commissioned by order of God our Savior and Jesus the Anointed, our *living and certain* hope), to you, Timothy, my true son in the faith. May the grace, mercy, and peace *that come only* from God the Father and our Lord Jesus the Anointed *mark your life.* (The Voice)

Christianity was never intended to be a "lone ranger" type of life.

In the book of Titus, Paul set out the duties of the younger and older members of the church. The older men were to be "sober, reverent, temperate, sound in faith, in love, in patience" (2:2). As men age, they often become set in their ways. Paul wanted them to be open to the ideas of men who are younger in the faith, and perhaps less experienced. Paul continued, "Likewise, exhort the young men to be sober-minded" (v. 6). Young men, and those young in the faith, are often impetuous and behave without regard for consequences. Paul would have them act in a manner becoming of their position in Christ. The writer of Hebrews emphatically stated that we are not to be "forsaking the assembling of ourselves together . . . but exhorting one another" (Heb. 10:25). Christianity was never intended to be a "lone ranger" type of life. We need one another, and in today's world, men need one another more than ever. They must come together to encourage, exhort, teach, and learn from one another.

It is interesting to note that, when Jesus chose the twelve apostles, He chose men of different ages, experiences, and occupations. John, the brother of James, was probably the youngest, and Bartholomew would be considered the oldest. The apostles were primarily fishermen, but we know that Matthew was a tax collector. Jesus set the example for a men's ministry to be intergenerational.

If your ministry doesn't have an intergenerational platform, you will be restarting your ministry to men every four to five years. Churches need to train younger men to get involved. Remember that it is not a program or event; it is the environment and culture that begins to reproduce mentoring (disciple-making) relationships.

It is interesting to note some of the statistics associated with males and why an intergenerational approach to ministry is so important:

✻ Seventy percent of all Ds and Fs are given to boys.

✻ Eighty-five percent of stimulant drugs prescribed throughout the world are prescribed to US boys.

✻ Boys have fallen behind girls in virtually every area of education.

✻ Boys are increasingly growing up with no compelling vision for manhood.

✳ Girls are outperforming boys in the workplace.[1]

An article written by Reverend Tim Wright and published by CNN iReport suggests that the church might be the best hope for boys. "The Founder of Christianity offers a vision for compelling manhood. Jesus offers boys a vision of what it looks like to be a man: Courageous, compassionate, a warrior against injustice, an advocate for the voiceless, a friend, passionate, committed, a man of his word, a man of action, gracious, humble, gentle, tough, forgiving, purposeful, commanding, strong, fully in tune with who he is, and ultimately a man willing to lay down his life not just for his friends, but for his enemies."[2] What better place for a young man to obtain a vision for manhood than through the mature mentors of the church?

Even the Catholic Church is having problems engaging with young adults. In 1996, the Catholic Church conducted a Life Survey and found that only 5 percent of Catholics aged sixteen to twenty-five attended Mass regularly.[3]

The men of the church need to reach out to younger generations who are often the by-products of broken homes, harassed environments, and a society that believes political correctness is more important than understanding God's plan for a man. Too many young men have a *father wound* because they have never had the blessing or encouragement from their father spoken into their lives. The *father wound* is created when men do not have a nurturing and loving relationship with their biological father. Even the strongest of men need the encouraging word and touch of a father. They often lack good role models in their lives and tend to be sucked into cultural norms made up of video games, gangs, and weak men. Is there any wonder why, at the age of eighteen, up to 80 percent of the males will leave the church? The church has a group of men who can pour masculine energy into the young people. The potential is only limited to the number of men willing to become participants and mentors in the lives of others, rather than spectators to a degenerating situation.

LET'S BE INTENTIONAL

One of my closest friends is retired Lt. Colonel Dr. Chuck Stecker, founder and director of A Chosen Generation and Center for Intergenerational Ministries. Chuck and his co-workers assist churches in developing intergenerational ministries with training and resources. One of the goals is to help the men of the church become leaders and mentors to the younger generations to help them build intentional intergenerational relationships.

When it comes to understanding and helping churches with intergenerational and cross-generational ministries, Chuck is the man. Dr. Stecker states, "We often confuse 'intergenerational' with multi and cross-generational. Intergenerational is not a program or a new ministry. Intergenerational is an 'environment' that intentionally grows relationships that cross generational boundaries and ways of thinking normally associated with one age group or another."[4]

Without an intentional approach to reunite the generations, church membership among males will continue to decrease until we become a place only for women and children. Our collective experience has shown that the steps listed below are needed to assist the church in its mission to bring together people of all ages.

Stecker also reminds us that, "Outside the church we are seeing a huge movement in the business community that already understands the need to connect generations for effectiveness. In addition, the greatest role model for 'intergenerational' ministry is the family. By design and by God's plan, the family is intended to be intergenerational."[5]

We must carefully explore ways to overcome self-centeredness and the entitlement mentality. Trust needs to be built over the mantel of time and patience. Understandings and relationships are formed once people are willing to be transparent and honest and to not judge others.

ASSESSMENT

As previously mentioned, the best way to determine the needs, gifts, passions, and interests of your men is to assess them. The Men's Ministry Survey Tool (Exhibit 2-A) should be given not only to your adult men, but also to your younger men who might not presently attend the regular men's ministry programs. Feel free to revise the Assessment Survey to seek out the ideas of younger men.

Make sure to include the young men in your senior high school, college, and the single men of your young adult and recovery ministries. After collecting the data, report back to these groups with your findings and invite them to help plan an event that resonates with their interests.

LEADERSHIP

Select one or two young men to be placed on your men's ministry leadership council. Consult your youth pastor for recommendations of guys who could be involved. Seek the involvement and support of younger men on the planning stage of a program. Remember that becoming an intergenerational ministry to men is a major paradigm shift. There may be some "push-back" from those steeped in an older approach to ministry. Intergenerational relationships are challenging but can be rewarding. Start slowly changing the culture, integrating more of the younger men's needs into your goals and objectives. Anticipate that there are risks and expectations involved that need to be managed and evaluated during the transition.

Some ideas that don't include and respect the values of older people may not be appropriate to implement. Making such a shift in program planning and implementation requires overcoming the individualistic mind-set that is so strong within both the very young men and the older men. Provide ways for them to plan and work together so they can value each person's perspective on life.

BALANCE WITH AGE-SPECIFIC MINISTRIES

Don't feel as though you have to be the end-all to every age group. It will be important to keep some age-specific activities while embracing a general intergenerational concept within the major men's ministry components (breakfast programs, retreats, special events, men's council, etc.). Where it makes sense, involve young men in the work of the ministry and then encourage them to participate. Different age groups need different entry points to become involved with ministry to men.

INTENTIONALLY INTEGRATE NEW IDEAS

It is better to start with integrating some small ideas or programs that have the highest probability of success. Men will need to warm up to the idea of having the mixed ages involved with simple events like a breakfast program. Most men like the idea of intergenerational activities, but the problem is that we just don't know how to do it. It will be difficult for the young or older men to even think about being transparent with one another during a sharing or prayer time.

One good method is to establish seating that breaks through age barriers, forcing the men to sit with those whom they might not sit next to otherwise. At a breakfast meeting, for example, set up tables that are based upon challenging topics—i.e., conflict resolution, coping with stress, or most embarrassing moments—then tell the men they are only permitted to discuss their chosen topic during the meal. But be sure the topic is a concern to all generations. Imagine some young guy trying to understand an older member talking about the effects of retirement or coping with social security, or the older member understanding what problems a young guy had with his girlfriend's Facebook page.

Just having the guys in the same room is a win! Let them involve themselves where and when it is safe to develop deep relationships. Unless it is a mentoring relationship one-on-one time, don't try and push more intimate encounters within a group setting.

CREATE INTERGENERATIONAL MOMENTS

Some of the programs listed on Exhibit 7 are perfect opportunities to experiment with intergenerational practices. Programs like a "Back to the 50s Classic Car Rally," or a "Servants with a Task Program Workday," or a Movie Night, or a Men's Night Out Program are good examples where mixing generations could be a lot of fun.

Ultimately, you want to design and encourage older and younger men to come together so that a mentoring relationship is formed. Most younger men would not feel comfortable just jumping into a mentoring relationship without first getting to know and trust an older man. Explore ways that older men could help the young guys with things like life transition issues and goal setting, or helping them learn how to maintain an automobile, change a tire, study the Bible, or do some household maintenance projects. The younger men can help the more senior guys learn how to handle social media issues, fix computer problems, or connect with their grandchildren, or even where to find young people for hire to assist with their yard work.

> Men relate best when they can sit side-by-side, focusing on external issues, so that freedom of thought without judgment can be experienced.

When you bring guys together, it is good to have them focus on external things, like changing a car tire, while discussing deeper issues. The idea is that face-to-face encounters can be scary. Review a movie when you are side-by-side, not face-to-face. Men relate best when they can sit side-by-side, focusing on external issues, so that freedom of thought without judgment can be experienced.

Outdoor activities (hunting, fishing, photography, archery, skiing) are great ways for mixing generations. There are special and exciting stories and memories to be built and shared in the outdoors. One of the newer ministries called Fathers in the Field helps guys connect and provides resources for boys of single parents who want a mentor.[6]

A GOOD EXAMPLE

When I first started in ministry, there was an older business leader who was about ready to retire. Bob was a mature Christian with a heart for mission work. We went out to lunch one day and he stated, "I really don't know what I'm going to do in retirement. I've sold this business and I think I'm going to get very bored without having a mission in life." Earlier he had told me that he just built a fully equipped large wood shop.

I thought for a minute and said, "What percent of the kids in your neighborhood live in a single-parent home?" Bob looked up from his bowl of soup and said, "I would guess about forty to fifty percent of the kids don't have a dad at home." I mentioned to him the idea of turning his shop into an after-school woodshop for these abandoned kids.

Within a month, he handed out flyers in the neighborhood and met with some mothers. In the beginning, he had around half a dozen boys show up on Wednesday afternoons at his shop. He told the mothers that he would be sharing a little Scripture, helping the boys develop their character, and encouraging them in their schooling.

> Bob invested his retirement;
> he didn't rock away by the fireside.

In addition to pounding on some small wood projects, the boys became fascinated with a computerized lathe Bob used for selected personal projects. He decided to award three minutes on the lathe for every Bible verse the boys memorized. Very quickly, the boys were operating the lathe, turning out projects, having some fun, and most importantly growing closer to Jesus.

Bob decided that they needed a group project to build the idea of team. He located some plans and supplies for a large canoe. It took months of work, but Bob and the boys built a beautiful canoe that was ready for a test in a nearby lake. Bob packed lunches for the boys and took them to the lake, and eventually hours of fishing, paddling, and fellowship became a common Saturday activity.

Within the context of their relationship, Bob became a good mentor and friend to these boys. And when he later died of cancer, the boys were at the funeral to share how their lives had been changed because an older man decided to re-fire his passions for the lost instead of retiring to a rocking chair with his Bible in hand.

BLUEPRINT FOR SUCCESS

Have you assessed your men to determine if various age groupings are being represented in the planning and implementation of your ministry to men?

What intentional steps has your ministry to men taken to include or meet the needs of younger men in your church?

What steps has your church taken to integrate the youth and young adults into your men's ministry program?

What activities from Exhibit 7 would best help connect the various age groups and interests of your men?

What action steps could be taken to improve the intergenerational mix of your church?

Have you thought about connecting with an organization like A Chosen Generation to assist the church in formulating a strategy to connect the generations?

BUILDING A PLAN

One of the first things your men's council can do is to place a young adult on the council board. Encourage the younger member to solicit ideas and comments from his peer group. Be willing to try some different ideas to better connect the older generation with the younger guys. Why not try a mixed-generation paintball fight, or develop a video game challenge whereby the younger guys have to teach the older men how to work a control and compete with other men in the church on a video game?

Try to develop programs that allow the older men to teach the younger men some practical skills, like changing a tire, budgeting, or business management skills. You will find that, after these generations work together, trust will be built that will lead to opportunities to communicate on more significant issues.

BIBLE STUDY

Read Acts 12:25 and 15:36–41.

☐ What caused the disagreement between Paul and Barnabas? Why did Barnabas want Mark to join them? Why did Paul refuse?

☐ John Mark was probably the person who wrote the gospel of Mark. How might Barnabas's treatment have influenced him in his life?

☐ Why did Paul take Silas with him after he and Barnabas parted ways? What do the priorities of Barnabas and Paul teach us about discipleship?

SO **WHAT** ARE **YOUR** **STRUGGLES?**

Too many men seem to have it rough in this world. They want to be the one in charge in their homes, but too many women are determined to be in control. They want to be respected, but often feel that the price is too high. They want to succeed in work, but discover that others have more drive and more connections, and are more willing to compromise. They want friendships with other men, but find it hard to move beyond surface subjects when they are with one another. They want to be good fathers, but their kids tell them, "I want this and that," and they can't get it all without working fifty to seventy-five hours a week. What's a guy to do?

All too often, they escape into work, alcohol, illegal or prescription drugs, pornography, adultery, computer games, or anything that leaves them isolated and provides only a short-term solution to a long-term problem. Then they begin to feel hopeless and wonder, "What's the use?" At this point, they attempt to rationalize or try to figure out what stressor they can eliminate. Many times these beleaguered guys decide it is the marriage; believing divorce is the solution to their problems. They can't quit work, and other activities give a small amount of pleasure. Also, they sense that the wife is not all that happy either. So, in rationalizing the situation, they decided that divorce would be a win/win situation. And the kids will adjust. They decide, "I just need [fill in the blank], and then I will be happy. And if I am happy, I can handle any other stress." If they are Christians and in an adulterous affair, sometimes they will even decide that "God wants me to be happy—and this other woman makes me happy." Of course, that goes against the entire weight of Scripture. God *hates* divorce (Mal. 2:16) for two reasons: first, it goes against His original design; and second, it hurts everyone involved—even generationally. Then they turn to other men for advice—and often to men who have been divorced. By the time they get around to consulting the pastor, they have already made up their mind to leave the marriage.

Take a look at this Barna report on divorce rates among Christian faith groups:

Denomination (in order of decreasing divorce rate)	% who have been divorced
Non-denominational	34
Baptists	29
Mainline Protestants	25
Catholics	21
Lutherans	21

Barna's results verified findings of earlier polls, that conservative Protestant Christians have the highest average divorce rate, while mainline Christians have a much lower rate. They found some new information as well: that atheists and agnostics have the lowest divorce rate of all. George Barna commented that the results raise "questions regarding the effectiveness of how churches minister to families." The data challenge "the idea that churches provide truly practical and life-changing support for marriage."[1]

Donald Hughes, author of *The Divorce Reality*, said: "In the churches, people have a superstitious view that Christianity will keep them from divorce, but they are subject to the same problems as everyone else, and they include a lack of relationship skills. . . . Just being born again is not a rabbit's foot."[2]

In this report, Hughes claims that 90 percent of divorces among born-again couples occur after they have been saved.

These statistics are not only sad and disheartening, but they are indicative that something must be done to preserve marriage, as it is one of the foundational, God-ordained institutions of our society. Where does one turn? Certainly not to the government. Hopefully, the church will step up and begin to find ways to heal broken marriages, restore trust, and provide encouragement to fight the good fight. The church, an institution designed and implemented by God, must learn to recognize and then reach out to the men who are having difficulties in their lives and learn how to encourage and support those men in their unique and varied battles. And if the church is going to be relevant in today's challenging world, then it must be about the business of addressing the top ten issues affecting men.

TOP TEN ISSUES AFFECTING MEN

FEMINIZING THEIR MASCULINITY

The twenty-first century is turning everything upside down. This is particularly true for men and the questions they ask. They feel confused, unappreciated, and even emasculated. A recent article in *The Telegraph* stated the following:

> Many men believe the world is now dominated by women and that they have lost their role in society, fuelling feelings of depression and being undervalued.
>
> Research shows the extent to which men have had to change within one or two generations, adapting to new rules and different expectations.
>
> Asked what it meant to be a man in the 21st century, more than half thought society was turning them into "waxed and coiffed metrosexuals", and 52 per cent say they had to live according to women's rules.
>
> What they apparently want is what some American academics have dubbed a "menaissance"—a return to manliness, where figures such as Sir Winston Churchill were models of manhood.
>
> The research also shows that just as women feel their work-life balance has been stretched to breaking point, men think they have too many roles to play.[3]

So, if this article is correct, where will they learn manliness? Men's Ministry Catalyst and other para-men's ministry organizations are dedicated to helping men be effective leaders in their homes, their church, their work, and their communities. It involves a process of knowing what men want and need, enlisting mentors for men and allowing them to be mentors as well as to be mentored, and teaching them what God's Word says about being real men. The program is predicated on the church being committed to helping men be who God intended them to be in every area of life. It takes time, work, and commitment, but what goal could be better for the church than to have strong, loving, capable men who are committed to Christ and living that out in their lives?

FINANCES AND CULTURE

At this point in our culture, when our nation is seventeen trillion dollars in debt and businesses are continuing to give out pink slips, men are concerned about how to support their families. Most men feel a deep-seated responsibility to care for the family. Again, the church can be of support. By having an effective men's ministry made up of men who know and care for one another, emotional, financial, and other kinds of support can be provided. Obviously, one way to get a job is by knowing the right person. Perhaps the men in the group can help others find work. Also, the men who understand finances and budgeting can sponsor a short program for the entire group on money management.

PORNOGRAPHY

Because of the Internet, pornography has become an epidemic problem for both men and women. However, look at some of the statistics just among men:

* Seventy-two percent of men have visited a pornographic site.

* Seventy percent of eighteen- to twenty-four-year-old men visit pornographic sites monthly.

* Sixty-six percent of men in their twenties and thirties report being regular users of pornography.

* Twenty percent of men admit to accessing pornography at work.

✳ Ten percent of adults admit to sexual addiction.[4]

So why do men watch porn? Kurt Smith, a marriage and family therapist, gives a number of reasons:

1. They enjoy sexual excitement and release, and porn delivers.

2. They like sexual variety, and porn has an endless selection to choose from.

3. In real life, the sexual practices that men like might not be those that their partners would like to engage in. In the world of porn, our sex partners will do anything we want them to do. And they will enjoy it. And they never get tired. And they are always ready for more.

4. The real world has a lot of stress and uncertainty. The world of porn is predictable and controllable.

5. In a world where men are all so busy with work, home, and family, a pornographic affair may seem like some small comfort for those who are cut-off and lonely.[5]

Here's another reason: it appears to be a victimless act. According to many men, no one gets hurt when they partake in online pornography. In fact, one can rationalize further that it is better to have an online affair than a real affair. And some men say, "What's the harm? She will never know." However, neither rationalization will hold water when held up to scriptural (and psychological) scrutiny.

There is a theory known as GIGO—garbage in, garbage out. What we put into our minds is what comes out in our actions.

> What we put into our minds is what
> comes out in our actions.

Jesus talked about the fact that, if you look upon a woman with a plan to commit adultery, you have already done so in your heart (Matt. 5:27–29). It is very difficult for the mind and body to differentiate between reality and fantasy. And the wife will know— she will definitely know that something is not right. A woman is incredibly intuitive about the man she loves. She especially is sensitive to the sexual relationship and can often sense when something is just not the way it was. Don't ever kid yourselves, men. God knows and eventually your wife will know too. And when she does find out, she will feel just as betrayed and hurt (and lose trust) as if you had been having a real affair. Here are just a couple of statistics on the effect that pornography has on marriage:

* Forty-seven percent of Christian families said pornography is a problem in their homes.[6]

* The Internet was a significant factor in two out of three divorces.[7]

This obsession with pornography is difficult to control without accountability and responsibility. Men need other men to keep them on the right track and to hold them accountable for their actions. They can encourage, discuss their own temptations, and help overcome this addiction. This type of interaction is, of course, best done with one or two male Christian friends.

DEPRESSION AND HOPELESSNESS

Depression is just one of life's unfortunate side effects in today's high-pressure world. It is not unique to men, of course, yet men can be somewhat more susceptible to depression because of our "pull yourself up by the bootstraps" mentality, combined with a lack of close friendships. One of the early symptoms of depression is chronic fatigue, or a nagging sense of "being blue."

> Men need other men to keep them on the right track and to hold them accountable for their actions.

And frequently, a man who notices these symptoms will try to compensate by working harder or taking some time off—as though work is the answer to all problems, whether more of it or less. But this leads to the man becoming irritable, withdrawn, and angry, and he loses interest in things that previously brought satisfaction. Studies indicate that church involvement is correlated with less depression and more family happiness.[8]

While I believe church is a major support to those struggling with depression, many times the depression is clinical and requires medication. It is not always a matter of changing one's thinking, and even church involvement and friendships *cannot* heal the clinical type of depression. One needs to seek out professional medical help to deal with the clinical or chemical imbalances associated with some forms of depression. For those struggling with depression, I recommend the following:

1. Seek out professional medical help and be open to their suggestions.

2. Encourage your church to openly address this issue. Talk to your pastor about bringing in Christian professionals who can discuss this topic.

3. Read Paul Meier's book on this topic. *Blue Genes* is perhaps one of the best works on the subject and has helped thousands of individuals. Also, Dr. Archibald Hart has many resources to help you better understand this complex issue.

4. Surround yourself with positive people and friends who will help you through the sad times.

5. Know that God will comfort and strengthen you through the process of discovery and healing. This includes getting the medical, spiritual, and psychological Christian counseling that will bring clarity to the situation.

Depression is deceptive in that it can go deep in a short period of time. Men begin to believe that there is no way out and they develop tunnel vision, which can lead to thoughts of suicide. They begin to feel hopeless. Also, their self-esteem is involved and, when they believe that they are no longer useful or have anything to contribute, there comes a sense that "everyone would be better off without me" or "I have to figure out some way to get out of this." Often, that way is suicide, even though it is irrational. In some times of depression, it does not appear to be irrational. It appears to be a solution. Of course, this is a lie straight from Satan. The following information, compiled by Mike Strobbe, analyzes some of the recent information on suicide:

> The suicide rate among middle-aged Americans climbed a startling 28 percent in a decade, a period that included the recession and the mortgage crisis, the government reported Thursday.
>
> The trend was most pronounced among white men and women in that age group. Their suicide rate jumped 40 percent between 1999 and 2010.[9]

Why did so many middle-aged whites—that is, those who are thirty-five to sixty-four years old—take their own lives? Some suggest that the recession caused more emotional trauma in whites, who tend not to have the same kind of church support and extended families that blacks and Hispanics do. The economy was in recession from the end of 2007 until mid 2009. Even well afterward, polls showed that most Americans remained worried about weak hiring, a depressed housing market, and other problems. Being unable to find a job or settling for one with lower pay or prestige could add that final weight to a whole chain of events.

BALANCE/STRESS

We live in a "get all you can" world—and get it quick—and get it better and bigger than the next guy. The drive to obtain things has resulted in living beyond our means, maxing out our credit cards, declaring bankruptcy, disillusionment, and a host of other consequences. Stress in our lives is creating the breeding ground for emotional, psychological, physical, and spiritual difficulties. We forget our priorities, especially as Christians. The drive to keep up with the neighbors creeps into our lifestyles. We want the latest toys; we want our wives to have the latest fashions or time-saving devices; and we certainly want our children to go to the best schools. We have great intentions and limited resources. As a result, we lose perspective and peace of mind. How do we recover? How do we maintain power, place, and face? Where is the balance?

We change. We reevaluate our life. We make very hard decisions. We begin to say no. We set different priorities. When this happens, men need support and affirmation and a strong will. We focus on the eternal—family, real friends, and our relationship with Christ. And when we decide to make changes, many people who we thought would support us can become our strongest adversaries. Some people hate change and will try everything and anything to get you back to where you were. And you must have men around you who will help, support, and encourage. The truth is that, when one person in a relationship (marriage, family, etc.) changes, everyone has to change. And the deeper truth is this: when the change is for the betterment of all, and you get to the other side of it, everyone benefits! The journey is difficult, but the end result is great (see Rom. 8:28).

You must have men around you who will help, support, and encourage.

FAITH

These topics inevitably bring us back to the basics: love, hope, and faith (1 Cor. 13:13). We work on the restoration of these three, and that means we must reevaluate and rearrange our lives. We focus on priorities and make the main thing the main thing. How much time are you spending with Jesus Christ and

His Word every day? What is your prayer time like? Is going to church and being with other believers something you look forward to doing, or are you just checking it off your list? Is Jesus real to you? Do you even know what faith looks like? Do you have that nagging feeling that something vital is missing from your life? That "something" is a close relationship with Christ because, when you have that, no matter what the outside circumstances look like, you can be at peace. And you and Christ can handle anything (Matt. 19:26; Phil. 4:13). It is difficult to do it alone. That is why we have fellowship with one another (1 John 1:7) and "shoulder each other's burdens" (Gal. 6:2 The Voice). It is our faith that undergirds us, gives us hope, and provides relevancy in an irreverent world. However, you must be involved with another male who will hold you accountable and encourage and support your life-changing decision.

RELATIONSHIPS

Count on your fingers the number of guys you could call at two in the morning to come and get you because your car broke down fifty miles out of town. How many? You are fortunate if you have one. By nature, most of us are hesitant to bother anyone. And yet, in many ways, that is what Christianity is about. We depend on one another; we lean on one another; we support one another; and we are there for one another. That is what we call *friendship*. We were not created to live or be alone (Gen. 2:18). The very concept of church is one of togetherness with other believers.

How does one go about developing true Christian friends? Getting into a solid men's ministry in a church would be one way to begin. From there, begin to get to know the guys and pick out someone you think would be a good mentor for you. Talk to that person about helping you grow as a man and as a Christian. Pray about a continuing relationship with that person. Friendships don't have to be forever. There are all kinds of friends— long term, short term, just for a season, forever. Express your need to grow, your expectations, and so forth. Get involved. Get committed—and go from there. It takes time and it takes work. But if you don't do it *now*, when will you?

INTIMACY

When you talk about intimacy, most men immediately think about sex. This is not about sex, but about being emotionally close to someone; about men with whom you can share your secrets, fears, hopes, dreams, failures, and successes; about having other men you can laugh with, cry with, and share life with. Too often, men view intimacy as being weak or feminine. That's not it at all. Maybe that's why men seem to prefer the term "brother" to "best friend." Perhaps the term "camaraderie" would be preferred over "intimacy." The truth is that being emotionally intimate with another man involves a great deal of courage, strength, and trust. It is not something men do on a regular basis. Men need the closeness of a friend-to-friend relationship with other men. Of course, it is always best to start off slow and develop trust. The important thing is that you begin the journey with someone who is spiritually mature and growing in the Lord, someone you respect, someone with integrity in every area of his life.

Why are men afraid of intimacy? Probably because they have been hurt at some point. It is interesting to note that women will often sit face-to-face with one another and share the deepest part of their lives. Men, on the other hand, normally only share with one another while they are doing something side by side. They experience things together; they accomplish things—that's success to a man. While they are doing those things, though, they can also begin to broach the elements of life that matter to them.

IDENTITY

The big questions of life: Who am I? Why am I here? Where am I going? Another one that follows closely on the heels of the others: Why does it matter? This is all about purpose. Do you have a purpose in life, or are you just drifting? Let's look at these crucial questions.

You are made in the image of God (Gen. 1:26). You were created because of the love of God and His desire to have a relationship with you (John 3:16). Why are you here? To use the gifts and talents God has given you to better yourself, your family, other people, and your world. You are here to grow to be more like Christ every day.

Where are you going? If you have recognized that you are a sinner (Rom. 3:23), have accepted Jesus as your Lord and Savior (1 John 1:9), and believe that God raised Christ from the dead (Rom. 10:9; 1 Peter 1:21), then you are going to live eternally with Him in heaven. Now, where are you going on this earth? Hopefully, you are going to continue to grow in the knowledge of Him who saved you, exemplifying His life to others, notwithstanding whatever else you may be doing. In order to do this, you must be involved in prayer, Bible study, Scripture memory, fellowship, and witnessing. A church with a strong men's ministry is the best

> A man of integrity thinks, acts,
> and reacts the same way as Jesus.

place to do just that. You need to find such a church and become actively involved in the work.

INTEGRITY

Integrity is such an important word, and yet, in today's world, it is losing ground and impact. When we look at various institutions and prominent individuals, we see a lack of integrity. We no longer have *statesmen*; we have *politicians*. When we look at various businesses, we see a lack of integrity. When we look at education, we see a lack of integrity. Our sports personalities often fail us because consistent character is lacking. A lack of integrity is seen any time someone is looking out only for themselves and cares nothing about others.

The word *integrity* comes from the Latin word *integer*, meaning whole or complete, and marked by moral consistency. The biblical concept of integrity suggests that a person is whole or complete because his character is consistent with the character of Christ. A man of integrity thinks, acts, and reacts the same way as Jesus. One old proverb tells us that "integrity is who you are when no one is looking."

And, on a less academic line, notice that the word "grit" is in the middle of inte*grit*y. It takes conscious choices to have integrity to do the right thing, especially when it is easier to take another road. But, like everything, it pays off in the long run with peace of mind. It's easier to have integrity when you have a person to whom you are accountable—a mentor, someone who will hold your feet to the fire and your nose to the grindstone in a loving manner.

SPIRITUAL APPLICATION

We are commanded to "love the Eternal One your God with everything you have: all your heart, all your soul, all your strength, and all your mind" (Luke 10:27 The Voice). Someone has said that "God is free, but He is not cheap." So, what does Luke 10:27 mean to you? This is something you have to work at to get the concept and then put it into action. Go on the Internet, check with your Bible study teacher, ask other men you respect, and pray that the Holy Spirit (the Counselor and Teacher) will instruct you as to how to do this—and watch God give the increase.

Exhibit 8 will allow you to identify some of your struggles and to apply biblical solutions based on what you have learned in this chapter to further explore a resolution to those issues.

BLUEPRINT FOR SUCCESS

For most men struggling with image and reputation, the John Wayne character is a myth. The reality is that men do cry, they feel the pain of life's disappointments, they struggle with identity issues, and men are fighting through the chaos of today to try and make a difference.

Sunday service isn't enough to float the sinking dreams, visions, and aspirations of many Christian men. Male participation in church activities continues to decline. I believe that unless our church culture changes, within a decade American Christianity will primarily be women and a few children like it is in many places in Europe.

If Christianity is to survive in America, it will take the church re-engineering its liturgy, worship, and programs to become more man friendly in its approach and practice. We need courageous pastors who not only are immersed in disciple-making theology but also care enough to be transparent and approachable to the men within their congregations. Spiritual Mentoring must become a primary focus within the church vision and practice.

BUILDING A PLAN

* Pray and determine to work on the places where you struggle. Tell God about them.

* Ask the Lord to bring men into your life to help you, as well as men whom you can help.

* Develop a dynamic ministry to men within your church.

* Commit to be a man of integrity in every area of your life.

* Pledge to learn to love God with all your heart, soul, strength, and mind, and put that into practice.

* Praise God in advance for His help and guidance.

BIBLE STUDY

Read Luke 10:25–37. What does it mean to love God with:

☐ all your heart?

☐ all your soul?

☐ all your strength?

☐ all your mind?

How is each of these things accomplished, in practical real-life terms?

BUILDING
INTENTIONAL
MALE
RELATIONSHIPS

THE LONELY MALE

The book description for *The Lonely American: Drifting Apart in the Twenty-First Century* by Jacqueline Olds presents a very bleak picture of our culture:

> In today's world, it is more acceptable to be depressed than to be lonely—yet loneliness appears to be the inevitable byproduct of our frenetic contemporary lifestyle. According to the 2004 General Social Survey, one out of four Americans talked to no one about something of importance to them during the last six months. Another remarkable fact emerged from the 2000 U.S. Census: more people are living alone today than at any point in the country's history—fully 25 percent of households consist of one person only.[1]

There appears to be a growing male population of the Baby Boomer generation (men born between 1946 and 1964) that manifest symptoms of depression due in part to feelings of isolation and loneliness. For many men of this generation, their focus on achieving and producing created a dynamic tension that was partially driven by their depression-era parents of "have nots." There was a push by parents that their kids should strive to be all they could be, to accomplish much with their education and talents.

> "Busyness . . . substitutes shallow frenzy for deep friendship."
>
> —**Chuck Swindoll**

After graduation from college, the drive to discover the American dream of being successful, happy, and financially secure consumed the schedules of most young men. Added to that was the nature of first-born conservative males who didn't properly prioritize their time to allow for the development of relationships. These individuals became so obsessed with having successful jobs, making money, being well known, and having things, that their families and faith got left behind, as did their ability and resources to develop lasting friendships.

Dr. Chuck Swindoll wrote, "Busyness rapes relationships. It substitutes shallow frenzy for deep friendship. . . . It feeds the ego but starves the inner man. It fills a calendar but fractures a family. It cultivates a program that plows under priorities. Many a church boasts about its active program: 'Something for every night of the week for everybody.' What a shame! With good intentions the local assembly can create the very atmosphere it was designed to curb."[2]

For some it seemed that the emerging American liberal culture of the 1960s and '70s was not a welcome place for a conservative young man of God. Once the younger Christian male generation left the protective environment of home, there was little motivation, time, or interest to develop meaningful friendships in a faith-based environment. Most Christian churches were putting their emphasis on the development of youth programs and forgetting about those who had graduated into young adulthood. Today, these men are the senior citizen populations within our communities.

The church still has done little to promote friendships within the sixty- to eighty-year-old population. They, like other institutions of our culture, have taken the transactional-analysis approach to helping older men cope with life—*if I'm okay, you're okay*. While many males of the Baby Boomer generation are now retired and available to serve, few have the spirit of camaraderie and team building that is necessary in identifying with the younger generations.

There are millions of lonely and emotionally isolated older Christian males in the church today. By the very fact that we love Jesus, we are already set apart from the majority of our culture who may see us as odd or eccentric. The apostle Paul reminded us,

> "So then turn away from them,
> > turn away and leave *without looking back*," says the
> > Lord.
> "Stay away from anything unclean, *anything impure*,
> > and I will welcome you." (2 Cor. 6:17 The Voice)

As children of the King, we are to be set apart; we are instructed to be in the world but not of it. That walk doesn't lend itself to the popularity of being part of "the gang," however. When the guys want to go to a strip joint for a beer after work, a Christian man would not want to join that group. Yet we want to be available to support and minister to that group when the opportunity presents itself. Let's look at what Christ said about our approach to the world:

> I have given them Your word; and the world has despised them because they are not products of the world, in the same way that I am not a product of the corrupt world order. Do not take them out of this world; protect them from the evil one. Like Me, they are not products of the corrupt world order. Immerse them in the truth, the truth Your voice speaks. In the same way You sent Me into this world, I am sending them. (John 17:14–18 The Voice)

A HEALTHY MODEL OF FRIENDSHIP

One of my favorite Bible stories is that of the deep and abiding friendship between Jonathan, King Saul's son, and David, the son of Jesse.

> By the time David had finished speaking to Saul, *Saul's son* Jonathan was bound to David *in friendship,* and Jonathan loved David as he loved himself. Saul took David *into his service* on that day and would not let him return to his father's home. And Jonathan made a covenant with David because he loved him as he loved himself. He took off the robe he wore and gave it to David, and also his armor, sword, bow, and belt, *symbolically transferring to David his right to ascend the throne.* (1 Sam. 18:1–4 The Voice)

Their friendship was so deep that, even when King Saul was trying to kill David, Jonathan remained faithful to his friend— and that is true friendship! According to Scripture, Jonathan was a little older than David and could have taken a totally different position with someone of lesser experience or rank. But

God had put it on Jonathan's heart to become a protector and encourager of David, even when it cost him a relationship with his dad. King David remembered this modeling as he wrote, "My father and mother have deserted me, yet the Eternal will take me in" (Ps. 27:10 The Voice).

King Saul became obsessed with trying to eliminate David. But out of respect to his friend Jonathan and his love for God, David stood firm on the Levitical law about revenge: "Do not seek revenge or hold a grudge against any of your people. Instead, love your neighbor as you love yourself, for I am the Eternal One" (Lev. 19:18 The Voice).

FRIENDSHIP—PART OF GOD'S PLAN

Beyond the obvious social value of friendship comes the heart of our loving God. God made mankind for fellowship—first with Him, then with one another. One of the things that sets humans apart from other creatures is the physical ability of language. Language is important because it represents one of the key ways that people connect to develop friendship. God's design for His people was freedom, building godly community, and relational fellowships that encourage and enrich one another to enjoy life abundantly.

Jesus taught His disciples that our top priority is fellowship: "The most important commandment is this: 'Hear, O Israel, the Eternal One is our God, and the Eternal One is the only God. You should love the Eternal, your God, with all your heart, with all your soul, with all your mind, and with all your strength.' The second *great commandment* is this: 'Love others in the same way you love yourself.' There are no commandments more important than these" (Mark 12:29–31 The Voice). Jesus told us to love our neighbor, but who *is* our neighbor? Your neighbor is anyone God places in your life. Your neighbor can be one who is a total stranger that you meet on the Internet or in the supermarket. What is true is that our acquaintances are men who need our support as much as we need theirs.

I travel a great deal. It is not uncommon that someone seated next to me in an airplane will ask me what I do for a living. When I tell them I'm an author and speaker, their next questions usually open the door of opportunity for me to begin a dialog about life. They will ask me what subjects I write about. We are not sitting face-to-face but shoulder to shoulder, and most of them believe we will never meet again—so deep conversations about a host of topics will be discussed. By the questions I ask, I can tell that many of these people don't have a close friend in their lives to chat about things that are bothering them. Once they get comfortable with our discussions, they tend to expand the conversation into areas that have real meaning to them.

ENCOURAGING MEN TO CARE

So often, conversations between males center around non-threatening topics like sports, weather, cars, hobbies, and so forth. Males typically are protective of their feelings and emotions. They believe that, if they let someone see their "underside," they will be judged as weak or insecure. So the typical response to "How are you doing?" is "I'm fine, how are you?"

Christ was tender, understanding, communicative, and loving. It is interesting to note that Scripture doesn't portray Christ as weak, effeminate, or without authority. On the contrary, a

God created us with a vacuum in our hearts for fellowship.

man who would toss tables around in the temple, chase people with a whip, rebuke storms, and face Satan head-on is a courageous and strong man.

God created us with a vacuum in our hearts for fellowship. He realized that, in our frailty, we would need others to help fill that emptiness. That is why He gave Adam his helpmate Eve and why He gives each one of us the opportunity to experience relationship. Given the number of men today who did not have a positive male role model in their home while growing up, I would conservatively estimate that at least 50 percent of the males I know have a "Father wound" or "Father vacuum" in their hearts.

The first step in healing the Father wound and moving toward a healthy relationship with other males is to confirm our identity with God. Instead of focusing on *who* we are (our drivenness, passions, work, pursuits), we need to rivet our attention on *Whose* we are. We are children of the King, joint heirs to the throne: "You no longer have to live as a slave because you are a child *of God.* And since you are His child, God guarantees an inheritance *is waiting* for you" (Gal. 4:7 The Voice).

In order to heal these wounds; conquer the spirit of oppression, abandonment, and rejection; and overcome our insecurities, we must confess our failures and wounds to God. By accepting the redeeming grace of our Lord Jesus Christ and understanding His love for us, we can better understand how much He loves us. We need to forgive those who have created the wounds within us that keep us from trusting others and enjoying intentional relationships. For me, confessing and forgiving is an ongoing process. At times when old tapes flash back in my spirit, it takes me back to my past and the disappointments I endured. When I think about being disrespected or taken advantage of, I become entrapped in the world of the flesh, which can translate into feelings of weakness, anger, and resentment. God plus the guidance and support of true friends can help me return to my spiritual stronghold.

"We need to provide opportunities for trusted men to intentionally invite young men into the transition of adulthood."

Changing my attitudes can also be a matter of focus. I can choose where I place my attention and thoughts. Do I want to be bullied by the negativity of the background noise in my life, or do I choose to place my attention on the things that strengthen me?

The church and intimate friends can help us with the processing of these thoughts. Godly men and struggling brothers can help us with things like the father's blessing that many of us did not receive. Through passage programs with our youth, we can be sure that no kid leaves the church without some significant male physically putting his hands on his head or shoulders and speaking a blessing of affirmation and hope into his life. As men of the church, we need to provide opportunities for trusted men to intentionally invite young men into the transition of adulthood. We need to be encouragers to one another. King Solomon had some wise words on this subject for us to consider: "Do not withhold what is good from those who deserve it; if it is within your power to give it, do it" (Prov. 3:27 The Voice).

FRIENDSHIPS WITH A PURPOSE

David and Jonathan modeled for us the ultimate friendship. Each knew that the other had his back. They encouraged the best in each other. Even when things seemed desperate, the friend was there to provide hope and support.

We need to pray for and find men who can help us become the best friends, husbands, fathers, and grandparents we were created to be. Through spiritual mentoring, wise counsel, spoken word, affirmation, and even at times rebuke and correction, we need responsive guidance and support to live a Christlike life. We need men who will not only help point us to the future but also be our comrade in arms by supporting our journey.

Once again, the church has a role in helping men make these connections. By providing safe and friendly environments, we can create an atmosphere and church culture where men can cultivate special friendships. As we previously discussed, opportunities like men's breakfasts, affinity groups, hubs, and Bible study groups are perfect environments to cultivate a spirit of transparency, trust, and respect that lead people to becoming vulnerable and build significant friendships.

We return to the example that David and Jonathan had in their relationship. David was a fearless hunter, a brave man, and a warrior (1 Sam. 16:18), and Jonathan was a leader who took his troops into battle (1 Sam. 14)—a common ground that helped knit their lives together to form a deep and abiding relationship. They shared common experiences and concerns. Their strength went beyond their visible position, physical stature, equipment, abilities, and fame; it was the inner commitment to support and encourage each other in intentional friendship that drew them together.

The commitment between David and Jonathan went beyond pleasantries; it became a covenant. A covenant implies an alliance, treaty, or union formed between two people, a holy bond that is not broken over differences of opinions, harsh words, or old wounds. The apostle Paul addressed this in his words to the Galatians, "For the whole law comes down to this one instruction: 'Love your neighbor as yourself,' so why all this vicious gnawing on each other? If you are not careful, you will find you've eaten each other alive!" (Gal. 5:14–15 The Voice).

Relationships that go beyond casual exchanges require a commitment of time, energy, forgiveness, and honesty. In a culture that has to have it now, real friendships are hard to come by. If we are going to change men—men who in turn will change our churches, who in turn will help change our culture—then we need to facilitate men coming together for cultivating and supporting the notion of building friendships that lead to the spiritual mentoring of one another and those they impact. It sometimes means correcting and admonishing a friend. When there is freedom to exchange criticism, friendships can be elevated to a whole new level. King Solomon said the same thing in a different way: "Wounds inflicted by *the correction of* a friend prove he is faithful; the abundant kisses of an enemy show his lies" (Prov. 27:6 The Voice).

Relationships take time, trust, and focus. As Paul said, "Finally, brothers and sisters, fill your minds with *beauty and truth*. Meditate on whatever is honorable, whatever is right, whatever is pure, whatever is lovely, whatever is good, whatever is virtuous and praiseworthy" (Phil. 4:8 The Voice).

BALANCE GIVING AND RECEIVING

Your life can only be in balance when giving and receiving are in balance. Every interpersonal relationship is built on this fact of life. He who always gives acts against this principle just as much as he who only takes. This basic truth is valid without exception everywhere people deal with people.

One of the issues that creates some dynamic tension between the younger and older guys today is that many younger men project a spirit of entitlement. To men who had to find their way in life through blood, sweat, patience, and tears, it is challenging to understand a young man who believes that he is simply entitled to have those things that took others generations to acquire or achieve. Thus, when a younger man has an expectation of receiving without giving or showing appreciation, many older men will rebel and cut short any opportunity for relationship.

> Your life can only be in balance when giving and receiving are in balance.

Many younger men find the older guys stuck on the past. More mature men forget about the excitement and rewards that come with seeking a new vision and exploring different ways to tackle an issue. Today social media has opened some unique doors to investigate and discover truth that can transform a life. Young men desire to have older generations appreciate their electronic world.

GET INTERESTED IN PEOPLE

Dale Carnegie once stated, "You can make more friends in two months by becoming interested in other people than you can in two years by trying to get other people interested in you."[3]

It is rare for someone in full-time ministry to be asked, "How is the ministry doing?" Unfortunately, too many people in ministry have utilized friendships to obtain resources, power, or connections. This has created distrust and an uncomfortable platform for some men to reach out to guys in ministry. The truth is that many guys in ministry desire someone to ask them about their day or work experience. There are many wonderful victories to be shared and miracles that would encourage others.

We need to resolve ourselves to intentionally focus our energy on helping others feel valued and appreciated. Show your appreciation with a thank-you or a smile. Men like to be asked about their occupations, hobbies, pastimes, and families. They relish telling you about their kids' activities and successes. Often these questions will become a bridge to develop other questions that will give you some insights into the person's struggles and feelings.

Too often men enter into conversations because they need something, and it ends up strictly as a business dialogue. Most people can detect a "need" conversation within minutes. When you call up someone you haven't spoken to in a while just to catch up on how they are, that becomes a special conversation. Building a friendship starts by genuinely caring for others.

BLUEPRINT FOR SUCCESS

It is so important to the health and vibrancy of our lives to have a good friend or two. As Chuck Swindoll stated so well, we have allowed the business of our schedules to consume us. Unfortunately, many of us wake up at the end of our careers and look around only to find emptiness. We haven't taken the time to develop those enduring and meaningful relationships outside of our work environments.

Consequently, many males face their depressions, failures, sin, and temptations without the wise counsel of a godly friend. God has put Himself in the hearts and spirits of men to reflect His Word and love. Imagine a friend who can flesh out the kind of compassion Isaiah wrote about:

> When you face *stormy* seas I will be there with you *with endurance and calm*;
> you will not be engulfed in *raging* rivers.
> If *it seems like* you're walking through fire with flames *licking at your limbs,*
> *keep going;* you won't be burned (Isa. 43:2 The Voice).

Who has your back? To have friends, you need to be a friend. Seek those godly friendships.

BUILDING A PLAN

Review Exhibit 9 and ask yourself if you are building intentional relationships.

✴ When was the last time you took someone out to breakfast or lunch just to check in on them?

153

* Can you make a list of three or four Christian men who share your passions and interests who might make good friends?

* Have you prayed about God leading someone into your life who could become that special buddy?

* Given your schedule and availability, what kind of time would you expect to pour into a mutually beneficial relationship?

* How can you manage the expectations that both you and a friend would bring to a relationship?

BIBLE STUDY

Read 1 Samuel 20.

How did Jonathan's friendship benefit David in this chapter?

How might things have ended differently if David did not have such a friend to depend on?

What did the friendship cost Jonathan? Why was Jonathan willing to pay such a price for David?

Men tend to look to women for validation. Doesn't scripture suggest we look to God's Word and our fellow brothers for validation (Rom. 15:2)?

THE **ULTIMATE MEN'S** MINISTRY TOOLBOX

"Rise up, O men of God!" If ever there was a time when men needed to heed those words, it is now. "Rise up, O men of God!" is more than a memorable phrase from a well-worn hymn or a carefully crafted slogan—it's a direct challenge calling men to stand their posts as spiritual leaders. As we have tragically learned, men are dropping out of church at an alarming rate. On any given Sunday, even to the casual observer, it will be noted that most church congregations are composed primarily of women. And those men who do attend a Sunday service would classify themselves as spectators, not participants.

In the movie *Braveheart*,[1] valiant warrior and patriot William Wallace, played by Mel Gibson, challenged his men not to turn their freedom into an excuse for complacency. He dared them to keep fighting the good fight for the values that had been entrusted to them. As he rode his white stallion up and down the frontlines of his discouraged troops, he admonished the men not to give up. Today our pastors and men's leaders need to imitate the passion and zeal of William Wallace in imploring men not to give up.

Currently, too many men are sitting on the spiritual bench in the dugout of life acquiescing as feminine control and leadership have overtaken many religious institutions in our culture. We have explored some of the reasons for the position men find themselves in today. Let's move to a more positive model and see what tools we need to develop an encompassing plan and movement that transcends the boundaries of traditional thinking in utilizing new messages, tools, and resources to get men into the fight for their souls and the souls of those around them.

Too many men are sitting on the spiritual bench in the dugout of life.

Thankfully, some men across America are rising up with a renewed determination to live as committed warriors of God in the midst of this conflictive culture. Some growing churches are seeing God's blessings as their dynamic men's ministries emerge and prosper. I just had lunch with a pastor who told me that the plan we outlined two years ago has taken hold of his men. He was excited to share with me the new direction his church is taking because the men are being discipled and making disciples.

Make no mistake; there is a long way to go in elevating men to the role God intended. Men's paraministry organizations are helping to lead the way in assisting churches with the goal of rebuilding the masculine, Spirit-led influence within the church, home, and workplace. And, if a guy is going to seriously work on any rebuilding project, he must have the right plans, tools, and resources to do the job. This chapter contains some biblical thinking that leads us to a variety of ideas, activities, events, and nuts-and-bolts resources for the purpose of helping guys form and deepen relationships with each other and with God.

Treat this book as a toolbox. Reach inside whenever you need an affirming message from God's Word, a design concept, a program model, specific help in accomplishing a ministry task, or to further your spiritual development.

Let's face it; most men are a little weird when it comes to reading directions. Sometimes men tackle projects without getting all the information ahead of time. Most users of this resource may read a section or chapter that is related to their area of responsibility without necessarily referencing some of the preceding conceptual building blocks contained in other chapters. That is why some repetition throughout this book is typically a good thing. Each chapter can stand somewhat on its own, thereby allowing a reader to jump into his task more quickly, but it is still foundational to read all the chapters and not just this one.

The missing link in the chain of successful men's ministry is the organizational structure that supports and embraces men's ministry. After more than three decades of experience, MMC found that the following development process works in almost every church size and culture.

Building an effective and dynamic ministry to men is one project men can't afford to put off. The stakes are too high to keep sitting back as observers or couch potatoes. Guys, let's rise above the failures, frustrations, faults, and fantasies, and become the Kingdom leaders God has ordained. So let's strap on the tool belts and get to work!

THE MISSING LINK

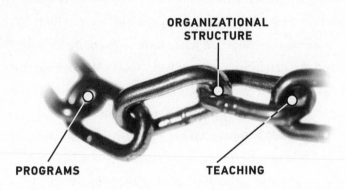

ORGANIZATIONAL STRUCTURE

PROGRAMS

TEACHING

In the early days of MMC, we endeavored to connect with men through a program-based model. Through men's retreats, father-child conferences, sports shows, hunting or fishing clinics, and a host of other outreach events, MMC sought to reach men through their passions and interest areas.

It worked—men who would not otherwise come through the front doors of a church were beginning to discover the importance of having a relationship with God and other believers. Many men sought out more and more of these "feel good" opportunities to become involved with faith-based program models that supported the Judeo-Christian values or early childhood faith experiences they endorsed.

Over the course of time, the original MMC (called Let's Go Fishing Ministries) helped birth almost a dozen other outdoor-oriented ministries that also provided many initial connecting programs for men all over the globe. Through the spiritual components of the regional workshops, clinics, retreats, and fairs, thousands of men deepened their relationship with and commitment to Christ. Unfortunately, too many of these men then went back to their local churches looking for encouragement but found that no effective or active men's ministry was present.

Another lacking component in developing men who came to faith through a program-based ministry was the lack of significant follow-up programs for new believers. MMC realized that, without a well thought-out discipleship (mentoring) program, those people who made an initial commitment to follow Jesus would soon fall away and become like the seed planted among stones in Jesus' parable of the sower (Matt. 13:5–6). Nothing of any value took root.

After the first five years (1981–1986) of ministry, much of the effort went into developing intriguing discipleship resources that helped a man connect his developing faith to specific biblical principles. New resources that were specifically designed to be practical and engaging to men who were not willing to read deep theological books about transformation were created. As the Holy Spirit continued to give us more insight on how to connect with men, we published our newest work on transformation that is the first book in this series, *The Spiritual Mentor* (Thomas Nelson, 2013). It provides some new thinking on how to approach discipleship in a vernacular that reaches today's man.

While discipleship should be the main focus of any church or men's program, it must be delivered in a method and structure where men can feel connected. The old method of a pastor or a wife simply giving a guy a must-read book didn't really motivate many guys to get involved with their faith because the books weren't either practical or motivational in their doctrine. In this book and *The Spiritual Mentor*, we have endeavored to present ideas within the context of relationship and useable ideas that can be easily applied to everyday living.

Today, there are almost one hundred parachurch men's ministry organizations whose purpose is to provide motivational speakers, programs, discipleship training, or curriculum to assist churches in equipping their men. They do a good job, and there needs to be a variety of men's organizations to work in the transformation process. Unfortunately, many churches do not have the vision, plan, power, staff, or dynamics to deploy many of the programs.

Too often, one or more of these elements becomes stagnant or fails because the proper organizational structure within the church does not enable a strategic vision and plan that would support and propagate an integrated men's ministry. To this end, MMC and a couple of other men's ministries have created proven models that specifically address the organizational structure needed to maximize the impact of programs, events, discipleship training, Bible study, and curriculum specific to men.

If ever there was a time when a fresh approach was needed to help revitalize men's ministry, it is now! Our experience has shown that less than 5 percent of the churches MMC has contacted describe their men's ministry as "vibrant and effective." By experience, MMC defines a "vibrant and effective men's ministry" as one that demonstrates the following traits:

✳ Men are directed to know God and make Him known.

✳ The pastor's vision and influence is incorporated into the ministry.

✳ There is a definable leadership council that meets regularly to pray and develop strategic plans.

* There is a specific emphasis on developing disciples of Christ.

* The focus of its service is on assisting the church in its mission to reach the world by becoming "salt and light" within their church, communities, and nation.

* They look for opportunities to financially support individuals and programs the church budget can't fund.

* Men are energized, empowered, and equipped to become faithful husbands and honorable fathers.

* There is a specific desire to provide multigenerational programs.

* The ministry is multifaceted and has many components that connect with men in a special way.

* Between 60 and 80 percent of the men are involved in the mission of the ministry.

For years, MMC endeavored to provide some of the best practices and programs contained within a men's ministry model. Many of these are listed in the exhibits at the back of this book. While MMC had great success in seeing thousands of men make an initial decision for Christ during an entertaining program, the reality is that most of these guys either went back to a vacant or ineffective men's ministry or didn't connect with a good Bible-preaching church with a dynamic discipling program.

Subsequently, considerable resources and efforts were given to developing resources and books on the subject of discipleship. Once again, MMC found that the materials, messages, and programs to assist many men and churches were initially valuable. Unfortunately, like the program component, once our ministry left the meeting, most churches did not, could not, or did not know how to continue to develop a successful men's ministry program.

Most parachurch organizations, like MMC, assumed that men knew how to develop a men's ministry. This was an erroneous assumption. The reality is that most men's ministries are run by volunteers who never really studied how or why a men's ministry needed specific Christian business models that were proven effective and that would create an atmosphere of practical learning and spiritual vibrancy.

Most men seem to better understand the dynamics of organizational structure if they can see it in a visual context. MMC believes the proven MMC development process for establishing a dynamic men's ministry looks like this:

MEN'S MINISTRY DEVELOPMENT PROCESS

RELATIONSHIP

| PILLAR 1 | PILLAR 2 | PILLAR 3 | PILLAR 4 |

———————— **DISCIPLESHIP** ————————

FOUNDATIONAL: GOD'S WORD & ASSESSMENTS

First and foremost, there must be a foundation built on a personal relationship with the living God through Jesus Christ. The Word of God is foundational to any process, program, or plan. The end goal is that men will be discipled and see relationships (both vertical and horizontal) as the by-product of a Christ-centered life.

Men cannot be directed or begin to define strategy until their interests, passions, goals, opinions, and leadership styles have been properly assessed. All the tools necessary to accomplish this are available in this book.

One of the foundations of MMC's men's ministry methodology is assessment. Ministries will rarely grow and improve if they don't periodically take time to assess how things are going. The following is an outline of the process that MMC recommends and utilizes to consult with scores of churches. With the assistance of a good men's ministry consultant, each of these pillars can be implemented and made part of the construction process of developing a vibrant men's ministry.

PILLAR 1: GOD'S WILL AND VISION

> Without counsel, plans go awry,
> But in the multitude of counselors they are established.
> (Prov. 15:22)

Pillar 1 speaks to the pastor's God-given vision for the church and how that connects to the men's ministry. An effective men's ministry program needs to make sure the pastor sees the value of a vibrant ministry to men that will assist him in growing the church and embracing, encouraging, and empowering his men.

The goal of a worthy men's ministry consultant is to help the pastor pray, plan, and execute his vision through an organized men's program. The consultant should work with the pastor and a church leadership team to initially assess, evaluate, develop, and deploy an appropriate vision statement. Sample vision statements can be found in Exhibit 3. Scripture tells us to seek the wise counsel of others (Prov. 15:22). Involve men from the congregation who are strategic thinkers. Identify guys who can help the pastor and consultant connect with the men in an authentic way. Men's ministry leaders need to instill within the men a positive vision and plan about the future of the ministry for their church.

PILLAR 2: MEN'S MINISTRY

> Take care of yourself, concentrate on your teaching, and stick with these things. If you do, then you will be effective in bringing salvation to yourself and all who hear you. (1 Tim. 4:16 The Voice)

Recruiting and nurturing leaders is critical to advancing men's ministry. The reality is that one man cannot do it alone. Most church men's ministry programs are primarily run by one or two guys who are passionate about spiritually growing the men of the church. Within twelve to eighteen months, these guys are burnt-out and over-stressed to the point that they eventually implode mentally.

Pillar 2 is about properly recruiting, training, and motivating a group of five to ten guys (men's council or leadership team) who see their primary mission as that of developing a strong men's program. The right men will unite behind a great vision and purpose.

> Building an effective and dynamic ministry to men is one project men can't afford to put off. The stakes are too high.

We see the men's council as the right arm of the pastor. They can implement the necessary surveys, strategies, training, and programs to keep the men excited about being connected with a ministry that is really doing something besides providing a breakfast program. By selecting a group of men with diverse backgrounds and skills who are united in purpose, the ministry can address the specific tasks associated with the organizational structure, including communications, marketing, program planning, budget, spiritual development, and crisis management.

The team approach to management is also found in many great companies. This approach allows an organization to take advantage of the particular strengths that each individual brings to the group. The key for the group is to properly delegate and deploy the strategies and plans of the council. The team needs to recruit volunteers who have a "get it done" mentality. Remember that enthusiasm is contagious! Men will rally around good leadership and positive projects.

Delegation with accountability is seen in Exodus 18:14–19. Moses' father-in-law, Jethro, encouraged Moses to delegate to others by finding the right men for the jobs. Most men are willing to give their time and resources to a job they can complete within their skill set, passions, and allotted time outside of their work, family, and community interests.

PILLAR 3: PLAN & CALENDAR

> To achieve this, you will need to add virtue to your faith, and then knowledge to your virtue; to knowledge, add discipline; to discipline, add endurance; to endurance, add godliness; to godliness, add affection for others as sisters and brothers; and to affection, *at last,* add love. For if you possess these traits and multiply them, then you will never be ineffective or unproductive in your relationship with our Lord Jesus the Anointed. (2 Peter 1:5–8 The Voice)

Pillar 3 is about leveraging and developing a specific plan and an annual ministry calendar. The plan deals with the *what, when, where, how,* and *who,* as well as the resources necessary to achieve the established goals. The plan also helps determine who will be recruited and how their gifts and talents can best be utilized for Kingdom work.

MMC's experience suggests that, when men see a vision supported by the pastor and a committed men's council that can establish priorities and create a workable plan and calendar, between 60 and 80 percent of the men will become committed to the effort. By participating, men will want to grow in their understanding of God's Word so they can be more effective leaders. Rather than the pastor trying to drive the Word into a few receptive souls, more men will seek God's knowledge and their pastor's messages so that they can be more effective in their specific tasks. Once a man steps into a leadership capacity, he knows that his personal Bible study and his prayer life must improve in order for him to be effective and competent in directing others.

The calendars identify specific targets for the pastor, men's council, and men's ministry. A balanced men's program includes a variety of specific opportunities for guys to get involved.

Examples of plans and calendars are available within the Tool Box located online at www.mensministrycatalyst.org/toolbox.

PILLAR 4: DYNAMIC EVENTS

> Whatever you heard me teach before an audience of witnesses, I want you to pass along to trustworthy people who have the ability to teach others too. (2 Tim. 2:2 The Voice)

Give men what they *need* in the context of what they *want* (passions, interests) delivered in an *approach* that produces *results,* and you will have begun the process of *transforming lives.* While Pillars 1–3 lay the foundation and organizational structure for a vibrant men's ministry, most men will see Pillar 4 as the place where they can participate. This is where the theoretical meets the practical. Through the men's ministry programs, there are numerous opportunities to:

* develop men spiritually;

* reach out to the community;

* implement and evaluate plans; and

* develop and deploy dynamic events and programs.

SPORTS MINISTRIES AND THE CHURCH

It should never be forgotten that true ministry is not about slick programs or clever approaches. It's about discipleship and relationship building, with the ultimate goal being to reach an unsaved population with the Good News. To be eternally effective, the end result of the ministry's focus must always lead people to God. To know God and make Him known should be the goal of every program. As in Christ's day, we need to target what distinguishes the audience and develop a prayerful strategy that helps build a bridge to better dialogue and deeper trust. The church needs to relate to others in more culturally relevant terms and provide programs that capture the attention of a lost community.

Jesus used many practical anecdotes and miracles to capture the attention of His audience and earn the right to be heard. So it is with Men's Ministry Catalyst. The many user-friendly concepts and program models found in this book and online will enable churches to build friendship bridges to a spiritually wary culture. In today's morally apathetic society, most people desire to focus on charisma and sensationalism instead of character. Men's Ministry Catalyst desires to encourage churches to utilize effective outreach models that project basic principles of first-century discipleship while encouraging Christians to utilize their spiritual gifts and talents.

> To be eternally effective, the end result of the ministry's focus must always lead people to God.

One tool that can be utilized from our collection of tools to involve men in ministry comes from our vast experience in outdoor sports ministry. Whether it is outdoor adventure programs like Fathers in the Field or the use of team sports like softball or basketball programs, a church can connect with men who might not otherwise come in the front door. Every outreach should have a time when you intentionally build relationships that can be followed up so that a mentoring process can be initiated.

A wide variety of feelings can be experienced in the great outdoors or on a sports field. Joy, fear, excitement, apprehension, wonder, exhilaration, and fascination are just some of the emotions one can experience while pursuing wilderness activities or participating in a field sport. And the outdoors provides numerous opportunities to interact with God's creation while evaluating individual strengths and weaknesses.

Many families have seen the memory-building moments that occur in the pursuit of activities such as hiking, camping, mountain biking, photography, or video-taping. There are millions of individuals in the United States who fish, hunt, or utilize archery as their primary area of outdoor interest. Many pastors and lay leaders alike have experienced the natural connection between people who enjoy the outdoors and those seeking to intimately know the Creator.

Dr. Roger Oswald, a long-time friend and founder of Sports Ministries International, reminds us:

> Sports activities as a gathering and interactive phenomenon produces its own unique harvest field. In Matthew 9:37 Jesus said, "The harvest is plentiful, but the workers are few." He was letting us know the relationship between farming and evangelizing. While some farmers raise wheat, others raise rice or corn. The harvest fields of the world are varied and scattered. The church has been good to recognize those and to be concerned for the "unreached" fields of the world— even concentrating financial and people resources to harvest those same unreached fields.[2]

Most churches do not see the untapped spiritual fields as people congregate to pursue their passions on the lakes, rivers, meadows, playfields, and mountains. Team and outdoor sports have become meeting places for millions who might not otherwise visit a church. Outdoor environments provide exciting opportunities for Christian participants to proclaim the gospel.

To penetrate a crowd, what better way than for one of the crowd to do it? To reach fishermen, what better way than to be a fisherman? The same is true with other areas of interests: hunting, cycling, hiking, skiing, and countless others. What did it take for God to reach us? It took the incarnation of Christ Jesus, who became the Ultimate Participant. Jesus wasn't a literal fisherman, but He cared about the things that fishermen care about—and in the eternal sense, He was the Master Fisher of Men.

PROGRAMS AND EVENTS

When used correctly, programs and events can strengthen the church in the following areas:

✳ A strategy for evangelization

✳ A tool for discipleship

✳ A means of fellowship

✳ A source of support

✳ A teacher of servanthood

✳ A trainer of leaders

✳ A maintainer

✳ A motivator of men

Men's Ministry Catalyst has utilized these events and many others to assist churches in creating dynamic environments for their men to grow while reaching unchurched men within the community.

EXAMPLES OF DYNAMIC EVENTS

Blueprints on the specifics of these programs are available by contacting us via www.mensministrycatalyst.org.

* Retreats

* Conferences

* Workshops

* Community help programs

* Character-building seminars

* Sports clinics

* Outdoor Adventure Fairs

* Fishing/hunting/golfing programs

* Car maintenance clinics

* Neighborhood assistance

* Tutorial programs

* Single-parent assistance

* Sports swap

* Sportsmen's archery clinic

* Special Kids' Day Events for the Disabled

* Happy Days' Revival/Show and Shine

* Get Hooked Outdoor Adventure Fair

* Summer church of the water

* Pro-sports outreach events

As we consider influencing men for Christ, we need to return to a process or plan that evokes and encourages men to engage with the church. The following diagram suggests one such process:

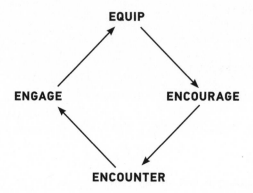

As we *encounter* men, we sometimes need to leave our comfort zone to *engage* them. Through a caring heart, acts of kindness, and purposeful interactions, we can *engage* men so they can be *equipped* with God's Word and specific resources that connect with their interest and passions. After they become equipped, they should be *encouraged* so they can evaluate their progress and believe that they have a real supporter in their new spiritual journey.

BLUEPRINT FOR SUCCESS

The best model for leadership was our loving Lord—how He managed, motivated, and directed His disciples in the elements that were important to the success and expansion of God's Word. Christ had many components to His leadership style, but clearly a few attributes stood out:

* He loved the people.

* He met people where they were and encouraged them to be the best they could be.

* He cherished the uniqueness of people.

* He was an encourager and inspirational figure.

* He made decisions based upon foundational principles.

* He modeled what He taught.

* He was transparent and available.

* He was an authority figure.

* He was effective and efficient in what He did.

* He was patient and principled.

* He was a teacher who motivated people to grow.

* He was patient and kind.

BUILDING A PLAN

When you consider working with men, how many of the above attributes do you bring into your leadership style? My good friend and fellow men's ministry leader Vince D'Acchioli, founder of On Target Ministries, gives a guideline to think about when working with men.

How did Christ work with men?

* He looked for them.

* He called them out.

* He led them.

* He taught them.

✳ He encouraged them.

✳ He released them to mission.³

In your ministry to men, which of these components have you implemented in your efforts to inspire and direct men? How could you better integrate these components into your different activities? List the areas, events, and programs in your ministry to men and see how many of the components you can place into future ministry. How does God gently challenge men to be their very best?

BIBLE STUDY

Read Matthew 13:3–8, 18–23.

☐ List the different types of spiritual soil that Jesus described in this parable, and give practical, real-life examples of how people today exhibit these traits.

☐ What "thorns" (v. 7) interfere with some people's response to the gospel? How can a men's ministry help to avoid those thorns when ministering to men?

12

IS CHRIST ALONE ENOUGH?

Among our close acquaintances, I can't think of any family that hasn't been touched by pain, suffering, or brokenness. It is part of life. From renowned pastors to everyday Joes, you will find families and friends with damaged relationships. Like a thief in the night the jarring disruption of betrayal, disrespect, entitlement, and discord can enter the most emotionally secure home. The emotional thief can steal the joy, peace, and comfort of a tranquil atmosphere.

Even our heavenly Father felt the pain of the brokenness experienced by His first family. The sons of Adam and Eve let jealousy, pride, and envy enter the doorway of their family. God said to Cain, "Why are you angry? And why do you look so despondent? *Don't you know that* as long as you do what is right, then I accept you? But if you do not do what is right, *watch out, because* sin is crouching at the door, ready to pounce on you! You must master it *before it masters you*" (Gen. 4:6–7 The Voice).

Anger, despondency, jealousy, and bitterness raised their ugly heads. Cain's envy toward his brother got the best of him, and he killed Abel. Think of the pain that God felt! Some of us have experienced a similar pain—when a spouse leaves a marriage for another person, when a son or daughter believes that drugs are the answer to finding joy, when an in-law disrespects your family values, when children no longer wish to walk with God. The list goes on and on.

SEEKING GOD'S PERSPECTIVE ON LIFE'S JOURNEY

In developing a dynamic ministry to men, it is critical that your men understand the brokenness surrounding them. Typically, men do not share the depth of their despair and pain with others. By developing a transparent and open environment, however, men can become more comfortable about sharing life so that they can receive the encouragement and support from those within the group.

Do you ever feel lost and alone? Often these feelings come about as a by-product of leadership. Someone once said, "It's lonely at the top." I'm no stranger to stress. I've experienced a variety of crisis situations, from surviving the outback after a plane mishap, to serving as a chaplain in the Katrina disaster, serving as a manager of a complex town, and tackling the challenges of ministry for over three decades. Each experience brings its challenges and potential for misunderstandings. Despite all my experience and scarred emotions, dealing with strife in personal relationships can still bring me to my knees quicker than anything else.

The inherent stress within our complex society stirs the pot of fragmented thinking and confusion that can become accelerators for pushing emotions and relationships between family members, friends, and church members into dynamic tension. No matter how much I wish it were different, unraveled relationships too often become burdensome and unfixable. Many tenderhearted church and ministry leaders I know have suffered from the vibrant tension of being a compassionate, loving man of God and working through difficult relational issues requiring tough love. At times, the pain within your heart can be wrenching and distracting.

> In developing a dynamic ministry to men, it is critical that your men understand the brokenness surrounding them.

The Old Testament prophet Elijah was a man who felt deeply. Despite his tremendous victory with God on Mount Carmel, he later allowed himself to be influenced by those who were attacking him. It was at Carmel that the prophet used the power of God to help put down the gods of Baal. He had taken a stand against 450 prophets of Baal and King Ahab and organized a "prophet duel" of sorts. While the odds were stacked against Elijah, he stood his ground and relied on the power of God Almighty—and God responded. He lit the fire that consumed Elijah's slain bull on an altar that had been soaked with buckets of water. A definite miracle had occurred before thousands of onlookers.

Elijah's faith and actions on Mount Carmel outraged Queen Jezebel. She ordered her army to hunt down Elijah and kill him. Elijah fled to the desert and began begging God to die. Fear and loneliness were all-consuming to this worried warrior. Despair filled the cave where he waited for his captors. In his depression, "he himself went a day's journey into the wilderness, and came and sat down under a broom tree. And he prayed that he might die, and said, 'It is enough! Now, LORD, take my life, for I am no better than my fathers!'" (1 Kings 19:4).

Elijah became more despondent and disheartened. He stopped drinking, eating, and exercising. Then God spoke to him, "What are you doing here, Elijah?" (v. 13).

Elijah poured out his grief to the Lord, and God encouraged him to go back the way he had come and enlist the help of others. God had already prepared seven thousand people who had not bowed down to Baal and would join Elijah, following the call of God upon their lives.

God knew that His prophet was feeling alone and overwhelmed, but He wanted Elijah to persevere. There was work for Elijah yet to do! When we're feeling alone and without direction, we need to answer God's question to Elijah: "What are you doing here?" God has you right where you are for a reason. He has a job yet for you to do—a job you're missing because you're too worried about "what's next" instead of "what's now." Sometimes the job God has for us to do right now is simply to wait. That is often the toughest assignment of all.

Those of us mentoring other men need to remind them that God needs and wants them involved in the battle. Satan attacks and distracts, which can render the most productive ambassador useless if we allow our hurts and pains to preoccupy our emotions, thus creating both emotional and physical handicaps that get in the way of being a conquering warrior for Jesus. Despondent guys need to realize that giving up isn't an option. Like Elijah, we need to physically rest, pray, listen to our encouragers, and, with the power of the Holy Spirit, move forward. As we pray for God's direction, let's remember to listen to His promises and review the past miracles and blessings in our lives. We never stand alone with God. He is our rock, our fortress, our redeemer, and our strength.

IS CHRIST ALONE ENOUGH?

When life deals us a lousy hand, and important relationships seem without hope, we need to reflect upon some of God's promises and encouragement. As mentors, we have a host of fulfilled promises and events from God's Word that can help encourage someone needing hope.

To the prophet Jeremiah God said:

> Blessed is the man who trusts in the Lord,
> And whose hope is the LORD.
> For he shall be like a tree planted by the waters,
> Which spreads out its roots by the river,
> And will not fear when heat comes;
> But its leaf will be green,
> And will not be anxious in the year of drought,
> Nor will cease from yielding fruit. (Jer. 17:7–8)

King Solomon, next to Christ the wisest man to ever live, gave us some parting thoughts to contemplate:

> My fruit is better than gold, yes, than fine gold,
> And my revenue than choice silver.
> I traverse the way of righteousness,
> In the midst of the paths of justice,
> That I may cause those who love me to inherit wealth,
> That I may fill their treasuries. (Prov. 8:19–21)

Isaiah wrote during the stormy period marking the expansion of the Assyrian empire and the decline of Israel, warning Judah that her sin would bring captivity at the hands of Babylon. During the storms that we face, God's Word is our comfort.

The LORD will guide you continually,
And satisfy your soul in drought,
And strengthen your bones;
You shall be like a watered garden,
And like a spring of water, whose waters do not fail. (Isa.
58:11)

And much like Elijah, David experienced the altering attitudes of a king, as King Saul, his friend and former encourager, turned against him. It was by experiencing the pain of rejection and despair that David wrote some of the most powerful and comforting psalms:

The LORD upholds all who fall,
And raises up all who are bowed down.
The eyes of all look expectantly to You,
And You give them their food in due season.
You open Your hand
And satisfy the desire of every living thing. (Ps. 145:14–16)

The message from God's Word is clear: we need not stand alone. Paul's teaching tells us that we can overcome much when we recognize and accept that Christ is with us in all we do:

I have been crucified with the Anointed One—I am no longer alive—but the Anointed is living in me; and whatever life I have left in this failing body I live by the faithfulness of

God's Son, the One who loves me and gave His body *on the cross* for me. (Gal. 2:20 The Voice)

BLUEPRINT FOR SUCCESS

How can we help men become more transparent? Can you imagine establishing a setting that invites people to begin to trust others? Everything from how we set up the room (round tables seating six to eight men), to the transparency of leaders around the tables, to the openness of the main speakers, to the follow-up after the meeting, will speak to men about a church that really cares for people.

The church needs to find ways to interact with men who are shy or withdrawn. Seeking ways to transcend preconceived notions about people who judge others is important to creating a safe and open environment where meaningful exchange of ideas can occur.

BUILDING A PLAN

Develop outreach events that allow guys to participate in ways that are welcoming and non-threatening. (See Exhibit 11 to make the most out of your event.)

Select men to lead the events and studies who are transparent and nonjudgmental. Intentionally target as leaders guys who have experienced the saving grace of Jesus after going through tough times.

Utilize Bibles and study materials that are man-friendly. The use of materials that have visual components are important to guys better comprehending and applying God's Word.

When a guy is in stress, depression, or despair, find a simple way to connect with him over coffee or an invitation to do something outdoors. Carefully and compassionately probe with open-ended questions that allow him to express his feelings and ideas. Become a good listener. Don't try and fix things as much as asking him questions that cause him to search for workable solutions.

BIBLE STUDY

Read 1 Kings 19. This passage took place soon after Elijah's famous confrontation with the prophets of Baal atop Mount Carmel (1 Kings 18).

☐ From a human perspective, why might Elijah have been discouraged and despondent after experiencing such a dramatic victory for God? When have you become discouraged or depressed after a significant accomplishment?

☐ How did God minister to Elijah? What did He do? What did He not do?

☐ What did God tell Elijah to do, once his spirits were lifted? Why was it important that he resume the Lord's work immediately?

13

MARKETING
MINISTRY
EVENTS

Sue Valerian helps us understand why marketing is so important to the health and welfare of a non-profit organization:

> Non-profits usually don't have a lot of money to spend on expensive advertising. But they do have a lot of interesting, compelling stories that are a natural fit for content marketing.
>
> That's why content marketing should be part of any non-profit organizations' [churches or men's ministry] marketing strategy. It's inexpensive and tailor-made for storytelling.
>
> So how do you get those stories—that content—out there?
>
> Blogs are one of the best ways to tell your stories to the public. You don't have to buy airtime on TV or ad space in the newspaper. You can blog right on your site for free.
>
> Do you have a story about how someone benefitted from your non-profit organization? Tell it in a blog.
>
> It's a genuine, compelling and an effective way to market your organization.
>
> Staff and clients are another good way to get a non-profit's story to the public.

They can post their stories on Facebook and tweet about their successes on Twitter.

A personal message about how an organization helped a client turn his life around or recover from an illness is a powerful content marketing tool.

It's also a way to make an impact on people who want to help, but might otherwise not know about your organization.

Compelling storytelling can help attract volunteers and generate donations and sponsorships.

We often hear about stories and videos "going viral" on the Internet. That kind of public interest can have tremendous influence and fundraising power.

Heartfelt stories in the news, too, can strike a chord with the public and get them reaching into their pockets to donate.

Just think: If a picture is worth a thousand words, could a story be worth a thousand dollars – or more?[1]

MARKETING IN A CHURCH

Marketing or promoting events and activities is essential in Christian ministry. If people don't clearly understand the concepts behind the event, they won't attend. And if they don't attend the activities and participate in the events, how are they going to grow spiritually? If you don't tell them, who will?

I've seen many examples of churches and men's ministries that have invested countless hours on praying, developing, deploying, and volunteering to provide a great event, only to have a few committed members show up. It is discouraging and disappointing to everyone involved. Also, it is a terrible waste of limited resources.

Unfortunately, most churches fear the use of the word "marketing." They falsely believe that, if the event is worthy of support, people will come. Marketing may be defined as "all the activity involved in the moving of goods, services, and information from the producer to the consumer, including advertising, packaging, selling, etc." In other words, marketing is *everything* that is done by a men's council or church front office to tell people about the vision, mission, plans, goals, objectives, and specific programs related to the men's ministry events.

We have the best "product" in the world. It has eternal value, it costs nothing, and it will never run out. A personal relationship with Jesus is worthy of our promotion and passion. A marketing program specifically designed for guys is one way to get the attention of men.

MARKETING DEFINED

Is marketing scriptural? Yes! A good example is found in Romans 10:

> "Everyone who calls on the name of the Lord will be saved." Faith is not something we do. It is a response to what God has done already on our behalf, the response of a spirit restless in a fragmented world. "How can people invoke His name when they do not believe? How can they believe in Him when they have not heard? How can they hear if there is no one proclaiming Him"? (vv. 13–14 and commentary, The Voice)

Marketing is key to this passage. Without telling people, they won't know; and if they don't know, how can they respond?

Scripture also makes reference to "gathering" people. And in order for people to gather, they need to be told when, where, and what for—and that's marketing. The following are several examples where people are told to gather:

> And Jacob called his sons and said, "Gather together, that I may tell you what shall befall you in the last days:
>
> > "Gather together and hear, you sons of Jacob,
> > And listen to Israel your father." (Gen. 49:1–2)

> And the LORD spoke to Moses, saying: "Take Aaron and his sons with him, and the garments, the anointing oil, a bull as the sin offering, two rams, and a basket of unleavened bread; and gather all the congregation together at the door of the tabernacle of meeting."
>
> So Moses did as the LORD commanded him. And the congregation was gathered together at the door of the tabernacle of meeting. And Moses said to the congregation, "This is what the LORD commanded to be done." (Lev. 8:1–5)

> The next Sabbath, it seemed the whole city had gathered to hear the message of the Lord. (Acts 13:44 The Voice)

Marketing events and activities do *not* happen by accident. They require careful planning, but do *not* have to be complex and time consuming. To effectively market events and activities, four actions are required:

✳ Establish a foundation for each event and activity.

✳ Review and implement sound marketing principles.

✳ Review and understand general marketing considerations.

✱ Develop and implement a marketing plan for each event and activity.

The information that follows addresses each of these four factors.

FOUNDATION FOR MARKETING

Getting people to attend and participate in an event or activity requires a marketing plan. The plan will utilize a strategy built upon sound marketing principles. In developing and implementing the plan, however, one must first establish a foundation on which to build the plan. The foundation is basic and simple. It requires answering three one-word questions: What? Why? and Who?

WHAT IS THE PRIMARY FOCUS OF THE EVENT?

This question is similar to the information presented regarding purpose. Is the purpose to try to do the work of evangelism (outreach), discipleship (training), church growth, or entertaining the men of the church? The response to this question may yield additional information useful in developing and implementing a marketing plan.

WHY ARE YOU HOLDING THE EVENT?

The purpose of the event will greatly influence the marketing plan. Therefore, identify and define the purpose carefully. For example, is the primary purpose of the event to promote fellowship within segments of the current congregation? Is the purpose to teach or train a current segment of the church congregation (e.g., parents, men, young boys)? Is the purpose to use the event to introduce the church to the community through programs like Men's Night Out, Outdoor Adventure Fair, or Movie Night? If there is not a specific purpose in mind for having the event, it is difficult to effectively market the event.

TO WHOM IS THE EVENT TARGETED?

What community or segment of the market is being targeted? Is the goal to reach men who wouldn't otherwise attend church? Or is it to impact a selected group within the church (e.g., young dads, teens, or single parents)? This is important to know, for it is good to market specifically to the target group. Using the shotgun approach to marketing, in which information is sprayed everywhere in hopes of attracting someone, is costly, time consuming, and very ineffective.

MARKETING PRINCIPLES

Having established the foundation for an event, it is now important to review sound marketing principles. For discussion purposes, a marketing principle is an element, consideration, or action that is essential for producing a desired result. And the desired result in marketing is for people to attend and participate in events and activities.

There are many marketing principles. The following have been selected for their relevance and significance to Christian events, activities, and programs:

The more leaders involved, the more it will draw support: When the senior pastor, staff, and lay leadership actively support an event

The key to marketing is identifying and using attention-getters that attract attention. It's like fishing: When the right bait is used in the right way, the fish are attracted and bite.

or activity, the congregation and members will feel that the program is worth supporting. When there is nominal staff support, few join the movement.

The more people involved, the better results it brings: Planning, organizing, and marketing an event or activity with one or two people generally doesn't produce good results. But a well-organized team can produce positive results. Therefore, encourage many people to get involved. When others are involved, the tendency is for even more to get involved. Each person has a separate and distinct network of associates who can support the program.

Wants and interests are a springboard to meeting needs: People participate in activities that interest them and give them what they want. Outdoor activities such as hunting, fishing, camping, golfing, and archery are of interest to many people. When people are offered something that will help them improve their skills and abilities while satisfying their wants and desires, they become connected with the program. Use interests and wants as a bridge to approach their spiritual needs.

People are attracted to successful and well-known personalities: If the springboard to meeting interests and wants is sports, then feature a Christian sports personality. If hunting, fishing, golfing, or camping is the attraction, have a recognized Christian

189

outdoorsman. Use the event or activity as an opportunity for people to hear and meet someone they would not otherwise get to see or meet in person.

Men are attracted to good food and plenty of it: When men know that good food is an integral part of an event or activity, they are more motivated to attend.

People like to get gifts and prizes: Door prizes can attract participation, especially if there are a variety of prizes, if the prizes are good in the eyes of prospective attenders, and if people know about the prizes in advance. These gifts do not have to cost money. Local merchants, church businessmen, and donors are most happy to participate.

Schedule events and activities when it is convenient for people to attend: Timing is critical in presenting events and activities. When the event is in competition with other events, you are likely

The best way to get people to attend events and activities is to promote a philosophy that "each one brings one." Posters, flyers, e-mail, telemarketing, radio, television, and newspaper announcements are good ways to market events and activities, and they should be used. The single best way to get people's attention is through personal invitation. The use of printed invitations or tickets along with a personal invitation encourages people to attend. Placing a monetary value on the ticket is a good way to get people's attention. They tend not to throw something away if there is a perceived value for the ticket.

to lose. Coordinate with the church, community, and school calendars to avoid scheduling conflicts. Also, don't forget to take into consideration the time and the season: hunting and fishing seasons, vacations, holidays, and the like can be competition to creating enthusiasm for the program.

People forget, so remind them: Remember, experience has demonstrated that the average man needs to be contacted three to four times before he will commit to attend a church function. Get folks to enter the date of the event in their calendars. But even when written down, it is still easy to forget.

An e-mail or phone call reminder just before an event or activity can be helpful: Postcards have good information, but they are *not* personal, and they can arrive too early or too late. The best reminder is still a face-to-face meeting or phone call a day or two before the event. Keep a list of those invited and call them. If they really want to go, they'll appreciate your reminder.

ELEVEN SUGGESTIONS FOR PUTTING MARKETING PRINCIPLES INTO PRACTICE

A successful event or activity is built around sound planning and a good marketing strategy. The following are suggestions for putting marketing principles into practice.

Discover the community. Find out what passions, hobbies, and interest areas the men in the community have, and then develop an event or activity that gives it to them.

From start to finish, *cover the event or activity with prayer.* This is the foundation of your strategy. Prayer will give the needed direction, support, and encouragement.

Gain the full and enthusiastic support of the pastor, other churches in the community, local service clubs, paraministries, like-minded organizations, and sportsmen's groups.

Involve the entire community, not just the church or organization. Have a key contact person in each church, club, ministry, and organization through whom to work and distribute information.

Form a team to plan, market, and conduct the activity, but have only the men's council members in charge of the primary program area. Use coordinators and committees to get work done.

Make the event so attractive that people can't stay away.

Make it easy for people to attend and participate. Select a good date, time, and location, and keep the cost minimal. When necessary, provide scholarships for men who cannot afford to come.

Analyze the event and develop a checklist to identify the details needed to make the activity a success. Men's Ministry Catalyst can provide a sample checklist that will help the director get started. It will need to be adapted to fit the specific activity and situation.

Establish a timeline. After making a checklist, it's a good idea to determine when tasks on the checklist need to be completed. In other words, take items on the checklist and put them in a time sequence in which they need to be done. Remember, plan well ahead. Don't wait until the last minute to get things done.

Market the event (tickets, invitations, radio announcements, newspaper articles, etc.) in a creative and attention-getting way. Make sure everyone knows about the event.

Record the event. Be sure to take plenty of pictures that can be shared with sponsors. Videotape the event as a learning tool and marketing resource for the following year.

GENERAL MARKETING CONSIDERATIONS

Along with a foundation and sound marketing principles, it's valuable knowing a few general considerations that make marketing a whole lot easier.

WORKING WITH OTHERS

Oftentimes, other groups and organizations in the community are interested in the same kinds of things that interest others. Here is a three-step approach to getting them involved:

1. Tell others about the event, activity, or program.

2. Tell them how they and the community will likely benefit from the event or activity. Create win-win scenarios.

3. Ask them for their support and involvement.

Involvement from others can make an event more successful, and it can make planning, promotion, and presentation easier too. Leverage the networks and resources of affinity partners. The following are groups and individuals to consider:

* Sportsmen's clubs (fishing, hunting, archery, camping, etc.)

* Pastor groups or pastoral associations

* Church ministry groups (men's, women's, youth, adult classes, home groups, etc.)

* Christian clubs and organizations

* Christian businesses

* Sporting goods stores

✳ Sports bars (Yes, this may be a good place to distribute information)

✳ Youth organizations (FCA, Young Life, Youth for Christ, Campus Crusade)

✳ Automobile and marine dealerships

DATABASE MARKETING

Leveraging a partner's e-mail database or direct mail database is mission-critical. It's a cost-effective way to multiply marketing resources and extend outreach. Explore what communication vehicles partners currently have in place and find ways to tie in the message with theirs. Consider leveraging their existing weekly or monthly communication vehicles so there is no need to reinvent the wheel when communicating with their audiences. Be prepared to offer a reciprocal arrangement with the database in the future.

MARKETING AND THE MEDIA

There are many opportunities to promote activities, events, and programs through print media, radio, and television. First, it is important to know how information is typically marketed to the public, and also how to get the media to market the information.

Each media outlet has a unique way of getting information to the public. Newspapers and free weekly publications typically present news and general interest information in a variety of forms:

✳ News columns

✳ Community interest or "perspective" features

* Editorials

* Club and Organization News

* Community Calendar

* Church page/Religion section

* Letters to the Editor (one of the most read sections of the paper)

* Paid advertising, classified and commercial

RADIO AND TELEVISION

Radio and television stations present information in a manner similar to the print media, but coverage is verbal (and visual) rather than written. There are several means by which events can be promoted through radio or television:

* A community calendar announces coming events and attractions, which can include a listing on the station's website.

* Public Service Announcements (PSAs) tell about upcoming events and activities.

* Talk shows discuss issues and activities of the community.

* Paid advertising can promote specific upcoming events (although it is expensive, and good results can generally be obtained without it).

* Television combines the verbal with the visual to present community calendars, PSAs, and news team coverage of events of interest to the community.

While it is important to know how an event or program might be promoted through the media, it's also important to know how to get the media to give you affordable or free coverage. There are two key things that are needed to help the media do its job:

1. Give them well-written information, well in advance, and in the format they prefer.

2. Provide information in the format that is common for your media.

What is the event and what are some of the important details?
Who is conducting the event and to whom is the event directed?
Why is the event being presented?
When is the event (date and time)?
Where is the event taking place?

From this information, a reporter or staff writer can prepare an informative piece. Further, the basic information may stimulate interest for more details and even photographs. When the media calls, have details ready and be available at their convenience.

Develop a relationship with the media. Make and maintain personal contact with the right people in the right departments. If the media doesn't know of the event and the leadership involved, their involvement will be minimal. Befriend the media and maintain an ongoing relationship with them throughout the year. Take them on a fishing, hunting, or golfing trip. Help them to feel special.

MARKETING WITH WRITTEN AND VISUAL MATERIALS

The marketing of an activity, event, or program can be greatly enhanced with attention-getting written and visual materials. Visual materials take the who, what, why, when, and where of an event and add color and illustration.

The key to visual materials is impact! Create attractive materials that viewers can absorb quickly. Because of size and space limitations, information generally must be short and to the point. People won't spend a lot of time reading a bulletin board, poster, or flyer. Also, an important consideration is to try and provide handouts, because quickly viewing something doesn't mean the information will be remembered. Therefore, produce materials in such a way that a person can cut it out, tear it off, pick it up, and take it home. The following are written and visual possibilities (many of which can be taken home):

* Tickets (even if there is no charge for the event)

* Discount coupons in newspapers and the like—some of the best results have come from placing ads in weekly community handouts or in the sports section

* Flyers with and without tear-off tabs

* Posters with and without information pockets

* Bulletin inserts

* Bulletin boards with and without information pockets

* Postcard invitations and reminders

* Banners

* Personal letters with tickets

✳ Video clips at meetings and services—make these exciting and dynamic

Samples of written and visual materials are shown in Exhibit 12.

DISTRIBUTING INFORMATION ABOUT YOUR EVENT OR ACTIVITY

Prior to the distribution of information, it's a good idea for event planners to review checklists and timelines to make sure the marketing plan is complete. If something is missed, there may still be time to include it (such as an insert in the Sunday bulletin or a mini-drama before the congregation). When everything is in order, put the plan in motion.

> Perhaps the most effective distribution of information is "each one reach one."

As stated earlier, perhaps the most effective distribution of information is "each one reach one." Most people will respond more positively to a personal invitation than to a broadcast message. Therefore, consider giving out packets of tickets and invitations to all those involved on the planning committee for personal distribution to friends, neighbors, and co-workers. Also, consider giving packets of tickets and invitations to Christian businesses and encourage them to personally give materials to customers.

The media, preparation, and distribution of releases to newspapers, radio, and television should be coordinated through one person, and the same is true for the preparation and distribution of posters and flyers.

BLUEPRINT FOR SUCCESS

As you can see, marketing is a key part of getting the message out. I hesitated for a moment about including this chapter in the book. I've never seen a person writing on spiritual mentoring talk about marketing. But when you think about it, wasn't that part of the plan when Jesus told His disciples to spread the Good News?

Maybe we need to find a more acceptable word in the Christian marketplace: publicity, mentoring with a plan, or _____ (you fill in the blank). Whatever it is, we need to be intentional about getting the word out to those who rarely attend church or read a bulletin or listen to an announcement. Part of growing a church is connecting with those who don't know what you are about. Spread the good news about your program for sure, but make it a practice to tell those outside your circle of friends.

BUILDING A PLAN

Gather influential members of your men's council and church board together and discuss the implications of becoming more intentional about your efforts to promote your church and program.

What would a marketing plan look like for your church and ministry to men? Can you imagine involving some of the people in your church who have sales and marketing experience in your discussions?

What if you brought in the young people to discuss how best to connect with others through social media? Can you imagine a viral marketing effort moving forward about an exciting event you have planned with a sports personality? How many people are in the network or friends list of all your junior and senior high church members?

How about abbreviating the pastor's Sunday sermon notes so that they could be sent to every member on Monday morning, that they might place them on their page of websites? See Exhibit 12 for some more ideas.

BIBLE STUDY

Read Matthew 28:18–20.

☐ What methods did Jesus command His disciples to use in telling people about the gospel? How do these methods compare with modern marketing techniques?

☐ Why is it important to tell others about Christ? Why is it important to tell others about upcoming men's ministry events?

ACKNOWLEDGMENTS

When Jesus said, *"Come,* follow Me, and I will make you fishers of men"* (Matt. 4:19 The Voice), He started a revival of spirit and hope that changed the world. Shortly thereafter, men began to gather together for worship and fellowship. Today, we call this fellowship *church.* Is the contemporary church really what Christ envisioned when He challenged men to take a leadership role within their families, their communities, and the world?

The ideas and resources available to the church are seemingly countless, yet oftentimes underutilized and unappreciated. Whenever you discover a vibrant church, you will usually find a dynamic men's ministry. The men of growing churches are engaged, committed, outreach oriented, and dedicated to seeking God's purpose in their lives. They understand the importance of encouraging and equipping other men in knowing God and making Him known.

In the apostle Paul's writings, we see him intermix the words *grace, gratitude,* and *thanksgiving.* In the Greek, these words share the same original root. So a heart filled with gratitude and thanksgiving recognizes that it is because grace has been extended so that we can give glory to God. Many people have extended much grace to me, and to all of them I say "thank you."

I honor the pastors and men's ministry leaders who understand why men are so important to the health and vitality of a church and a home. Leaders, we appreciate and acknowledge each of you. The staff and board of directors of Men's Ministry Catalyst are to be commended for their support, encouragement, and assistance to churches with best practice strategies, program models, biblical analysis, and innovative resources that help build great disciples.

A special note of appreciation is given to our hardworking and dedicated headquarters staff. No man is an island, and no relevant author can work in a void. I'm very blessed to have gifted and dedicated people surrounding me. A writer needs safe places to exchange thoughts and test new paradigms. Thank you to James Steiner, Whitney Steiner, Brandon Aldridge, Tim McWhorter, Dr. Karen Johnson, and especially my lovely and faithful wife, Louise, for giving me the time and effort that has helped create this unique project. May God richly bless each of you!

I truly appreciate the men's ministry friends and men's ministry colleagues who faithfully serve our Lord by utilizing their gifts and talents. Their contributions to my life and the development of men's ministry are a key to the success of reaching men for Jesus. I'm reminded of the words of William J. Bennett: "Thinking of friends and their worth is often enough to drive away an army of fears, regrets, and envies."[1] During the many long days associated with the development of this project, I was thankful to have the support and understanding of several friends and family members. I especially want to call out Pastors Chuck Swindoll, Jim Putman, Kent Mankins, and Daryl Kraft for their wise counsel and encouragement.

Finally, I wish to thank Columbia Evangelical Seminary and Dr. Rick Walston for the encouragement they gave me in preparing the initial work from which this project was based as part of my doctorate degree.

Faith is not something we do. It is a response to what God has done already on our behalf, the response of a spirit restless in a fragmented world. "How can people invoke His name when they do not believe? How can they believe in Him when they have not heard? How can they hear if there is no one proclaiming Him?" (Rom. 10:14 The Voice).

EXHIBITS

EXHIBIT 1-A
A REVIEW OF MEN'S MINISTRY MODELS

HOW TO AVOID THE 37 COMMON FAILURE POINTS

There is no shortage of models for creating men's ministry. Some leaders evaluate the effectiveness of their men's ministries by the number of activities they have in a year. Others wish to see more Bible study programs. Still others evaluate their ministries on whether or not they are "organic." There are various ideas as to what "organic" means.

Why do some men's ministries succeed, while others continue to fail no matter what ministry model they try to emulate? Success or failure is not necessarily determined by what works, but by what has failed to work in most ministries. By eliminating the common failure points that cause most ministries to be a disappointment, a pastor can find ways to achieve a very successful program.

Once again, MMC believes it is important to underscore the key to making any men's ministry successful. It must be a ministry that intentionally directs men to loving God and loving one another. It is about helping to transform men into the likeness of Christ. That is accomplished through a discipleship process that is inclusive and not exclusive.

Most of the following common failure points could have been avoided if the pastors and men's leaders created a vision and plan that addressed the previously mentioned focus. In more than three decades of experience, MMC has found some commonality among men's ministries that had failed or did not have a strong presence in the church. The following list is meant to assist pastors and leaders in assessing their men's programs. The solution for each of these problems is contained in the body of this book and in the resources that are recommended.

MEN'S MINISTRY COMMON FAILURE POINTS

How many of these failure points are seen in most men's ministry? The 37 Common Failure Points are broken down into four general categories.

1. GOD'S WILL AND VISION

✳ Pastor's vision is not integrated into the men's programs.

✳ Men's ministry is a low priority for the church in terms of time and money invested.

✳ Men's leadership is in denial about needing help with men's ministry.

✳ Most men's ministries don't use proven practices and, therefore, fail or don't get started because of the "it wasn't invented here" mentality.

✳ Fear of failure: men do not want to fail.

✳ The average pastor has many fears and apprehensions about how to structure and execute men's ministry programs.

✳ Some pastors fear that the active men will take over the church and replace the pastor.

* Many pastors have concerns and fears of being totally transparent with their men.

* Generally, pastors have not received adequate training in the area of leadership development, organizational structure, and business management. They need to know how to supplement their experience and delegate tasks (Ex. 18:13–23).

* An environment is lacking where guys can share their hearts, fears, and passions.

2. THE MEN'S MINISTRY

* The men's council is not working. They are committed and knowledgeable but have no bandwidth to execute the plan.

* The men's ministry leader is mistaken in his thinking that, since *he* doesn't have the need for outside coaching and tools, *others* don't need to be equipped either.

* Men's ministry leaders are solely focused on the immediate plan and tasks, and disregard developing longevity in the leadership team and building a leadership legacy.

* Men feel left out if they can't see the pathway from brokenness to significance.

* Most pastors think that men's ministry will take up too much time and money.

* The wrong people have been picked to lead the ministry— they don't have the proper skill set or spiritual gifts.

* Leaders of the men's ministry are not engaging and enthusiastic. There are not enough younger, spiritually mature men to go around. Pick a man's man to be the leader.

✶ A safe environment is not provided for men. What is said in the room must stay in the room. Safe environments need to be enforced or have a meaningful purpose.

✶ A person can be a great man of God and a great teacher, but he might still not be a good men's ministry leader.

✶ It is rare to have a significant population of men who have leadership skills above the pastor's leadership level.

✶ Men's ministries that are not relationship-based are often event-based or just rely on what the "good old boys" want to do or have always done.

✶ Without a church council (leadership team) committed to the pastor's vision and setting priorities, problem solving doesn't happen.

✶ When men don't pray and play together, they don't stay together. Provide ample times for both.

3. THE PLAN AND THE CALENDAR

✶ There is frustration about how to select the most effective model for men's ministry.

✶ Practical content does not exist.

✶ Leaders make it complicated. Instead, keep it simple!

✶ Men's priorities and schedules are not taken into account. Leaders ask men to do meaningless tasks and do not respect their time.

✶ There is not enough structure to the program: What? When? Where? Who?

* Men want to know that someone has properly researched the game plan.

* Men fail without a plan or vision. Great ministries have one-to five-year plans in place that provide good organizational structure and detailed program planning.

* A calendar of events has not been fully developed.

4. THE PROGRAMS

* Men's ministry is just a clique for the spiritually mature. It should be open to all, including the broken.

* Little or no opportunities exist for evangelism or outreach. Without a passion for outreach, men do not become engaged.

* Men are turned off by ministries that aren't challenging, compelling, adventurous, risk-taking, and dynamic.

* Unsuccessful ministries forget the importance of being multi-dimensional and intergenerational in nature.

* Churches that do not reach out to their church body (single parents, youth, and seniors) or do not become involved with community benevolence programs usually become intro-verted and more like country clubs than effective ministries.

* A heart for evangelism and discipleship is not found in the core values of the unsuccessful men's ministries.

EXHIBIT 1-B
IDENTIFYING THE CRITICAL COMPONENTS FOR EFFECTIVE MEN'S MINISTRY

Effective ministry to men requires:

1. Having a clear and definable vision.

2. Developing specific and measurable goals and objectives.

3. Assessing the needs and interests of your men.

4. Creating a hospitable and non-threatening environment.

5. Providing biblically relevant teaching and training opportunities.

6. Committing to building relational and friendship bridges.

7. Addressing real-life needs with the truths of Scripture.

8. Scheduling a variety of ways that men can enter the church and connect with other men.

   —Conferences and retreats

   —Special events

   —Equipping seminars

   —Community outreach programs

   —Small groups

   —Bible studies

   —Hobby and sports groups

   —Intergenerational events

The primary goal of an effective men's ministry is to strategically help men transfer biblical truth into personal commitment by providing the necessary environments for men to make and keep their promises to Jesus Christ, as well as their families, friends, churches, and communities.

EXHIBIT 2-A
MEN'S LEADERSHIP SURVEY

We desire to provide our church with a progressive and vibrant Men's Ministry Program. Please fill out this form so that we can discover your skills and interest areas to help us build our Men's Ministry leadership team. When ranking your answer, (1) is low and (10) is high. Thank you.

GENERAL OVERVIEW

1. How would you describe where you are on your spiritual journey (check one)?

   ☐ Questioning the "truth," i.e., religion and God

   ☐ Growing in my relationship with Christ

   ☐ Investigating truth and a relationship with Christ

   ☐ Mature in my faith and looking to serve

   ☐ "I'm a Christian, but don't feel like I'm growing"

2. How would you describe your involvement at this church (check one)?

   ☐ New attender

   ☐ Regular attender/member

   ☐ Occasional attender

   ☐ Highly involved attender/member

3. On a scale of 1 to 10, how would you evaluate your experience in leading men's ministry?

1   2   3   4   5   6   7   8   9   10

4. One a scale of 1 to 10, how would you rank your knowledge of God's Word?

1   2   3   4   5   6   7   8   9   10

5. What is your desire for this Men's Ministry?

6. What is your passion or major interest area?

7. What are your spiritual gifts? (Check as many as apply.)

☐ Discernment

☐ Prayer

☐ Deliverance

☐ Encouragement

☐ Help

☐ Administration

☐ Teaching

☐ Serving

☐ Healing

☐ Mercy

☐ Other: _____

☐ Don't know

8. What type of work do you do?

9. Please indicate your skills/experience/comfort level in the following areas:

Planning/Strategy: _____

Organizing: _____

Outreach: _____

Writing: _____

Graphics: _____

Phone calling: _____

E-mail communication: _____

Greeting/welcoming new people: _____

Computer support (Word, Excel, PowerPoint, etc.):

_____

Food prep: _____

Database administration: _____

Other: _____

10. How much time could you allot per week to participate in Men's Ministry?

- [ ] 1 hour per week
- [ ] 2 hours per week
- [ ] Project based
- [ ] Other: _____

11. What topics would most interest you? Add a "P" if you would participate or an "H" if you would be interested in helping lead.

- [ ] Accountability
- [ ] Prayer: corporate and personal
- [ ] Healing
- [ ] How to be a Christian in the workplace
- [ ] How to be a better husband
- [ ] Gifts of the Holy Spirit
- [ ] How to be a better father
- [ ] Sexual ethics
- [ ] Principles of godly financial management
- [ ] Discovering God's will for your life
- [ ] Evangelism/outreach
- [ ] How to have quiet time with the Lord
- [ ] Serving
- [ ] Raising godly kids
- [ ] Discipleship/mentoring

☐ Discovering your spiritual gifts

☐ Maintaining a strong family relationship

☐ Other: _____

12. What program area(s) would most interest you and to which you'd invite a friend? Add a "P" if you would participate or an "H" if you would be interested in helping lead.

☐ Retreats—Onsite and Offsite

☐ Woodworking Group

☐ The Gathering: Men's Community Bible Study Program

☐ Guys Movie Night

☐ Family Conferences & Camps

☐ Father/Child Outing or Camp

☐ Sportsman's Outreach Banquet-Breakfast

☐ Men's Retreat

☐ Outdoor Adventure Fair

☐ Sporting Event

☐ Boyz and Their Toyz

☐ Fishing Outing

☐ Men's Night Out Program

☐ Hunting Trip

☐ Sportsman Show

☐ Regional Men's Rally

☐ Father/Child Programs

- [ ] Super Bowl Party
- [ ] Pistol Club
- [ ] Sweetheart Banquet
- [ ] Special Kids' Day for the Disabled
- [ ] Adventure Travel
- [ ] Promise Keeper Group
- [ ] Disaster Preparedness
- [ ] SWAT Team (servants with a task)
- [ ] Boating/Water Ski Adventures
- [ ] Golf Group
- [ ] Snow Ski Adventures
- [ ] Clinics: Archery, Fishing, Hunting, Football (Outdoor Skills workshops and training sessions)

13. What resources would be the most help to you in growing your faith?

- [ ] Teaching
- [ ] One-on-one meetings
- [ ] Interesting books
- [ ] Written materials
- [ ] Small group meetings
- [ ] Short stories
- [ ] Videos or DVDs
- [ ] E-mail devotionals

☐ Studies on CD

☐ Electronic magazines

☐ Other: _____

YOUR CONTACT INFORMATION

Name: _____ Title: _____

Address: "City, St, Zip": _____

E-mail: _____

Phone #: _____ Cell #: _____ Work #: _____

COMMENTS

_____

_____

_____

_____

_____

_____

_____

_____

_____

_____

_____

_____

_____

_____

PRAYER REQUESTS

EXHIBIT 2-B
MEN'S MINISTRY/MEN'S LEADERSHIP JOB DESCRIPTION

There are many different models for leadership. MMC's experience tells us that an effective men's ministry must have dynamic leadership and a vision for discipleship. Most important to any effort is relationship. The following are characteristics associated with a vibrant men's pastor, men's ministry leader, and men's council leadership team. It would be almost impossible for anyone to have all these qualities, of course, but MMC recommends that these gifts be demonstrated in the team surrounding the individual leader.

Leader	Team	Quality
X	X	Manifest the Bible qualities identified in Timothy and Titus
X	X	A "discipler of men"
X	X	Relational in nature
	X	Filled with grace and mercy
	X	Not judgmental
X		Good verbal communicator
X		Willing to be a team player
X		Encourager
X		Extrovert
X		Organizer
X		Risk taker
X		Healthy family; supportive wife
	X	Loves being around guys
	X	Basic computer skills
X		If not full-time, willing to give an average of 2–3 hours per week

Leader	Team	Quality
X		Visionary
X	X	Willing to support vision of senior pastor
X	X	Teachable spirit

EXHIBIT 2-C
MEN'S COUNCIL LEADERSHIP AGREEMENT

Throughout Scripture, we see good and poor examples of leadership. A document like this one can be a great tool in helping your team to grow spiritually and better define specific responsibilities. Typically, men like to be challenged and appreciate accountability.

The following spells out the minimum requirements to be involved with the Men's Council.

☐ **Spend regular time with the Lord** (in personal prayer and study of the Bible). *Psalm 119:99–105; Hebrews 4:12; 1 Peter 2:2*

☐ **Discuss my involvement in ministry with my wife.** Prioritize my life; I will not let men's ministry become a burden to my family and will seek to be a good steward of my time. I will strive for balance between home, work, and ministry. *2 Corinthians 4:18; Philippians 2:2–5; Hebrews 12:1–2*

☐ **Each Council Member will have a specific area or team** which they are responsible for engaging and assisting.

☐ **Work toward unity in the leadership team.** Specifically, this means . . .

- When I encounter conflict, I will first search my heart and God's Word to filter emotions. If I have a problem with another person, I will go to him directly. *Proverbs 12:18; Matthew 7:12; James 1:19*

- I will pray for the other men on the team and build them up with genuine words of encouragement, and offer help when appropriate. I will strive to make my words life-giving. *Colossians 2:2–3; 3:12; 1 Peter 2:17*

- I will refrain from gossip. *Psalm 19:14; Proverbs 10:19; 16:28; Ephesians 4:29*

☐ **Be hopeful.** I will demonstrate a positive perspective and always assume the best in situations. *Nehemiah 8:10; 2 Corinthians 10:5; Philippians 4:4; Hebrews 11:1*

☐ **Be in a small group.** I will seek to emphasize spiritual growth and accountability. I commit to being transparent and real on the Men's Council and give permission for those I serve with to hold me accountable. *Psalm 19:7–11; Philippians 1:9–10; Colossians 3:16*

☐ **Commit fully to my specific responsibilities.** To the best of my ability, I will attempt to attend all scheduled meetings and events. *Proverbs 10:9; Colossians 3:23–24*

☐ **Attend church on a regular and non-compromising basis.** *Psalm 95:6–7; Romans 15:5–7; 1 Peter 2:9*

☐ **Be "outreach oriented."** I will refrain from being judgmental and will show grace and mercy to others. *Matthew 22:37–39; Galatians 6:10; 1 Peter 1:22; 1 John 3:17–18*

☐ **Enter into ministry with a "Learn, Do, Teach" Approach.** With this mentoring mind-set, I am ensuring that the ministry does not revolve around or rest on me, and that it will continue after I am no longer a part of it. Within ninety days of my end date, I will find my replacement who will have council and pastoral approval.

Learn: 2 Timothy 2:2; Do: 1 Timothy 4:7–9; Teach: 1 Timothy 4:10–13.

☐ **Seek to follow Christ's example.** I will integrate a servant leadership approach by leading with humility, being ready to serve, and doing even the smallest tasks to help any event or ministry happen. *John 13:1–17*

☐ **Tithe 10 percent of my income to the Lord.** And regularly give additional offerings to Men's Ministry collections as I feel the Lord's leading.

☐ **Report immediately to the Men's Council any major moral failures.** These may include infidelity in a marriage, an arrest, or other major sin area that is hampering your focus on God's leading in your personal, professional, or ministry life. This moral failure may lead to stepping down from the council, either temporarily or permanently, as decided by the senior pastor or church elder.

Name: _____

Service Start Date: _____

Service End Date: _____

Signature *(If applicable)*: _____

Today's Date: _____

Spouse's Name: _____

EXHIBIT 3
DEVELOPING A VISION AND MISSION FOR AN EFFECTIVE AND DYNAMIC MINISTRY TO MEN

The Lord tells us that, without proper plans, our efforts will fail. Developing a vision for your ministry to men is extremely important. "Plans fall apart without *proper* advice; but with the right guidance, they come together nicely" (Prov. 15:22 The Voice). "Whatever you do, do it as service to Him, and *He* will guarantee your success" (Prov. 16:3 The Voice).

PHASE ONE QUESTIONS

1. What is the vision for this church?

2. Do you really know your culture?

3. Do you have a vibrant men's ministry program?

4. Why do we need a men's ministry?

5. What is your model for men's ministry?

6. Is your men's ministry program reaching outside the church?

7. How are they reaching others?

8. What is your vision for this men's ministry?

VISION SETTING PROGRAM

The following definitions and examples will assist the pastor and men's ministry leaders in formulating a philosophy for your men's ministry program.

VISION STATEMENT: WHO AND WHAT; OBJECTIVE OR TARGET

Vision is the ability to see or envision something in the imagination or a dream. It should be far-reaching and attainable in the distant future. The statement should guide anyone seeing it to the major emphasis of the ministry. It should be inspiring and engaging. Many churches have the statement relate to the mission statement of the church. What is the big-picture idea or hope for your ministry?

SAMPLE STATEMENTS

✱ To provide strategic men's ministry opportunities that will grow men in our church and share Christ's love in tangible ways in our community.

✱ To provide opportunities, specifically for men, to fulfill God's five purposes in their lives of worship, fellowship, discipleship, ministry, and mission.

✱ (Your ministry) inspires, equips, and encourages men and their families for discipleship and church outreach that leads to greater opportunities to serve and lead others.

✱ To provide a multifaceted men's ministry program that will help change a community while inspiring the men of (your church).

* To help turbo-charge the faith of men in (your church) to reach the world for Christ, one life at a time.

* To build Christlike character within individuals affected by the work of (your church).

* To inspire the men of (your church) with a vision to affect their community for Christ.

* To encourage discipleship and help build strong families.

TAGLINE: SHORT STATEMENT OF VISION; SLOGAN

Sample Statements:

* Making Men's Ministry Happen

* Equipping Men, Serving God

* Loving God, Engaging Men

* Equipping and Encouraging Men for Outreach and Discipleship

MISSION: HOW WE GET THERE—A TASK THAT A PERSON OR GROUP IS SET TO PERFORM

How will you accomplish your vision? Utilize the Mission Statement to empower the men toward some details of the vision.

Sample Statements:

* To help train and empower men in the areas of discipleship, evangelism, and community service

* Using biblically based information, provide a multifaceted approach to discipleship, evangelism, and biblical family values

✱ To equip men in becoming Christlike in character while having a sensitivity toward their community

✱ To use an intergenerational approach to mentoring men spiritually

GOALS AND OBJECTIVES: HOW, WHAT, WHERE, WHEN— TIME-DATE STAMPED WITH BENCH MARKS

These should be specific statements of what is to be done, where it should happen, and the timeline associated with the event. This can be the area where specific programs are mentioned.

Sample Statements:

✱ We will have monthly men's council meetings to pray, plan, and execute effective men's strategies and ministry.

✱ We will have four quarterly outreach events every year.

✱ On a monthly basis, we will utilize our ministry to assist the widows and single mothers of our church.

✱ We will have a monthly men's breakfast emphasizing discipleship training and mentoring.

✱ We will provide strategic men's ministry opportunities that will grow men in our church and share Christ's love in tangible ways in our community.

PROGRAM AREAS: A SAMPLING OF SPECIFIC PROJECTS AND PROGRAMS THAT CAN BE INCLUDED IN A MEN'S MINISTRY PROGRAM

✱ Sportsmen's Gatherings; Outreach to the community

✱ Leadership Training on Discipleship and Lifestyle Evangelism

* Men's Fraternity/Accountability Groups
* Summer Church on the Water
* Pro-Sports Outreach Events
* Monthly Men's Breakfast
* Annual Sportsmen's Breakfast
* Quarterly Men's Night Out
* Men's Bible Study and Prayer Meetings
* Safety Patrols for Local Trails
* Happy Days Revival/Classic Car Rallies
* Get Hooked Outdoor Adventure Fair
* Follow-Up Discipleship Program
* Sportsmen's Archery Clinic
* Special Kid's Day Events for the Disabled
* Men's Weekend Retreat
* Men's Golf Tournament
* Sports Swap

EXHIBIT 4
MEN'S COUNCIL BEST PRACTICES

COUNCIL MEETING OVERVIEW

We recommend meeting at least once a month, with twice a month being ideal. Most men can only attend one meeting per month. We recommend something like the first and third Tuesdays of each month from 6:45 to 8:00 a.m.

If events are upcoming, don't overwhelm your men with tasks. It's helpful to stage the work involved and spread it out over multiple meetings.

Continue to measure and evaluate your goals and objectives. The meeting is not the place for the work to be done. Each crew leader should work with his sub-committee on the details of their specific tasks.

The council should be as much about prayer and addressing needs of men in the church as it is about planning events or developing programs.

The council meetings should also be used as a time of sharing, healing, and prayer for the men of the council. Since the men on the council are leaders in the church, many times they don't have a comfortable place to get godly input on and prayer for their own needs, largely because they are dealing with the needs of the church.

Once every four meetings or so, go around the table at the start of a council meeting and ask each council member how he is doing. This can lead to healing moments as the guys who are the pillars of the church receive some of the holding-up that they are so used to giving others.

Develop and distribute a contact sheet with phone and e-mails of all Men's Council Members, including their wives' names. This will help facilitate more personal contact. You might want to include e-mail addresses and birthdays too.

COUNCIL MEETING

Make sure to assign someone to bring coffee, donuts, or fruit. Help to make it friendly and a way for a guy to catch a snack before going to work.

Start on your knees. Hold the meeting in a place where you feel comfortable actually getting on your knees to uplift one another.

One of the men should be selected to take notes. Ask for a volunteer. Ideally it should be someone with a laptop or mobile device who can take notes electronically during the meeting.

Within forty-eight hours of the meeting, distribute the minutes to the team and copy the senior pastor.

SAMPLE AGENDA

✱ Open in prayer: gather requests; go around the table to have men pray for one another and for others in the church. Encourage men to fully participate. It is often advisable, at least in the beginning, to ask men to write out prayer requests for future meetings.

✱ Scripture verse for the day

* Old business

* New business

* Finance report

* Assess progress toward vision, plan, and purpose

* Pastor's update (Every month, someone in the group needs to take the pastor to breakfast or lunch and determine what needs, concerns, or problems he is having and how the men's ministry can help.)

* Communication efforts: e-mail, print, telemarketing; review feedback and plans

* Volunteers (database): review progress in capturing info, disseminating it to appropriate people, etc.

* Review the feedback from volunteers.

* Discuss upcoming programs and projects: get volunteers if necessary

* Closing prayer

OPTIONAL AGENDA ELEMENTS

* Men's Council book study (on church leadership, MMC resources, etc.)

* Plan activities to do together outside of meetings: play times/ team-building; quarterly dinner out, include spouses as appropriate

QUARTERLY IDEAS

✷ Talk about the roles/job descriptions on the leadership team and progress in mentoring other men in these areas

GENERAL COUNCIL MEETING TIPS

✷ The meeting time is also about relationship. It is important to develop accountability, so don't take the entire time for task items.

✷ Use humor. Keep things fun as you challenge and encourage guys to stay on task and meet goals and objectives.

✷ Before you leave the council, find your replacement (subject to review and approval from council and pastor).

EXHIBIT 5
HOW TO IDENTIFY THE TRUTH ABOUT MEN TODAY

When it comes to ministering to men, it's important to define the goals and objectives. Just as we wouldn't exasperate ourselves by using a wrench as a hammer to build a home, we need to understand the unique challenges associated with reaching men today. Here are the realities associated with men in this culture and why they are ripe for harvest:

* Most men are friendless.

* Men tend to be emotionally isolated.

* Men are commonly confused about their leadership role in the home and church.

* Most men would say they are spiritually searching.

* Many have regrets about how little time and energy they've spent on being a good husband and dad.

* Men tend to have guilt about the lack of focus on spiritual values.

* Most men see success as the primary goal in life, not significance.

There is a pre-occupation with money, sex, power, and position. It can leave little time for faith and family.

EXHIBIT 6
MEN'S MINISTRY CONGREGATIONAL SURVEY FORM

We desire to provide our church with a progressive and vibrant Men's Ministry Program. Please fill out this form so that we can discover your interest areas and bring others to Christ.

We appreciate your help! And while we'd love to implement everyone's ideas, without people to lead various events and activities, they will only be considered suggestions.

Prayer Requests

_____

_____

_____

_____

_____

General Overview

1. How would you describe your current church involvement (check one)?

☐ New attendee   ☐ Regular attendee/member

☐ Occasional attendee   ☐ Highly involved attendee/member

2. How would you describe where you are on your spiritual journey?

☐ Questioning the "truth," i.e., Religion and God

☐ Growing in my relationship with Christ

☐ Investigating truth and a relationship with Christ

☐ Mature in my faith and looking to serve

☐ I'm a Christian, but don't feel like I'm growing

☐ Other: _____

3. What are your passions/hobbies? Please list.

_____

_____

_____

4. What topics would most interest you, or to which would you invite a friend? Or, if you would be interested in leading, please mark LEAD.

	Participate	Lead	No Interest
Recovery—substance abuse, pornography, gambling, etc.	☐	☐	☐
Prayer: corporate and personal	☐	☐	☐
Faith in the workplace	☐	☐	☐
Healing	☐	☐	☐
Gifts of the Holy Spirit	☐	☐	☐
How to be a better husband	☐	☐	☐
Sexual integrity and purity	☐	☐	☐
How to be a better father	☐	☐	☐
Discovering God's will for your life	☐	☐	☐
Godly financial management	☐	☐	☐
How to have a quiet time with the Lord	☐	☐	☐
Evangelism/Outreach	☐	☐	☐
Raising godly kids	☐	☐	☐
Serving	☐	☐	☐
Discovering your spiritual gifts	☐	☐	☐
Discipleship/Mentoring	☐	☐	☐
Maintaining a strong family	☐	☐	☐

Other: _____

5. Have you been aware of activities or opportunities specifically for men at our church?   ☐ Yes   ☐ No

6. Would you like more information on attending a weekly men's gathering/Bible study if the time was convenient for you?

☐ Yes   ☐ No

7. What type of work do you do? _____

8. What are your spiritual gifts? _____

☐ Serving   ☐ Prophecy   ☐ Administration

☐ Mercy   ☐ Teaching   ☐ Faith

☐ Exhortation   ☐ Evangelism   ☐ Compassion

☐ Giving   ☐ Pastor   ☐ Hospitality

☐ Knowledge   ☐ Wisdom   ☐ Don't Know

☐ Discernment   ☐ Leadership

☐ Other: _____

9. Please indicate areas in which you have a high degree of skill/experience/comfort:

☐ Planning/Strategy   ☐ Mechanical

☐ Organizing   ☐ Computer support (Word, Excel, PowerPoint, etc.)

☐ Outreach

☐ Writing   ☐ Food preparation

☐ Graphics   ☐ Database administration

☐ Carpentry   ☐ Greeting/welcoming new people

☐ Phone calling

☐ E-mail communication   ☐ Musical skills (vocal or instrumental)

☐ Marketing   ☐ Social Media/Networking

☐ Other: _____

10. How much time could you allot per week to participate in Men's Ministry?

☐ 1 hour per week   ☐ 2 hours per week

☐ Project based   ☐ I have a lot of time available; please contact me

☐ Other: _____

11. What program area(s) would most interest you, and to which
    would you invite a friend?

	Participate	Lead	No Interest
Retreats Onsite and Offsite	☐	☐	☐
Father/Child Outing or Camp	☐	☐	☐
Saturday Men's Bible Study and Breakfast	☐	☐	☐
Golf Group	☐	☐	☐
National Men's Conferences (Iron Sharpens Iron)	☐	☐	☐
Family Conferences/Camps	☐	☐	☐
Sportsman's Outreach Banquet/ Breakfast	☐	☐	☐
Attend College/Pro Sporting Event	☐	☐	☐
Guys Movie Night	☐	☐	☐
Outdoor Adventure Fair	☐	☐	☐
Fishing Outing	☐	☐	☐
Regional Christian Men's Events	☐	☐	☐
Hunting Trip	☐	☐	☐
Mission Trips	☐	☐	☐
Regional Men's Rally	☐	☐	☐
Father/Child Programs	☐	☐	☐
Super Bowl Party	☐	☐	☐
Pistol Club	☐	☐	☐
Sweetheart Banquet	☐	☐	☐
Men's Retreat	☐	☐	☐
Adventure Travel	☐	☐	☐
SWAT Team (servants with a task)	☐	☐	☐
Disaster Preparedness	☐	☐	☐
Boating/Water Ski Adventures	☐	☐	☐

	Participate	Lead	No Interest
Clinics: Archery, Fishing, Hunting, Football, Baseball, etc.	☐	☐	☐
Snow Ski Adventures	☐	☐	☐
Wood Working Group	☐	☐	☐

☐ Other: _____

Your Contact Information

First Name: _____ Last Name: _____

Phone #: _____ Cell # _____

Work#: _____ E-mail: _____

Address:

City: _____ St.: _____ Zip: _____

Age:

☐ <19   ☐ 30–39   ☐ 50–59

☐ 19–29   ☐ 40–49   ☐ 60+

Marital status:

☐ Never married   ☐ Presently separated

☐ Married, first time   ☐ Divorced and single

☐ Married, second time   ☐ Widowed

☐ Other: _____

How would you like to be notified about men's activities?

☐ Phone   ☐ E-mail   ☐ Facebook

☐ Text   ☐ Regular mail   ☐ Announcement

Comments (we welcome your feedback on anything)

_____

_____

_____

_____

EXHIBIT 7
INTERGENERATIONAL PROGRAMS

* Attending Sporting Events

* Car Maintenance Clinics

* Woodworking Classes

* Neighborhood Assistance Workday

* Tutorial Programs

* Sports and Swap Day

* Archery or Shooting Clinics

* Happy Days Revival - Revisit the '50s and '60s

* Outdoor Adventure Fair

* Summer Church on the Water

* Paintball Games

* Video Games

* Social Media Workshop to Help Grandpa Stay Connected with Grandchildren

* Football Parties

* Movie Night at Church

* Men's Night Out Programs

Details for these and other intergenerational church programs can be found by contacting www.mensminstrycatalyst.org.

EXHIBIT 8
SELF-EVALUATION

On a scale of 1–5 evaluate what issues are the most difficult for you to deal with. What are some of the things you can do to obtain support on coping with these struggles?

Top Ten Issues Affecting Men	Not an issue	Could be a problem	Have identified this as a problem	Weekly struggles	Daily struggles
Struggle:	1	2	3	4	5
Finances and Culture:	1	2	3	4	5[4]
Pornography:	1	2	3	4	5
Depression and Hopelessness:	1	2	3	4	5
Balance/Stress:	1	2	3	4	5
Faith:	1	2	3	4	5
Relationships:	1	2	3	4	5
Intimacy:	1	2	3	4	5
Identity:	1	2	3	4	5
Integrity:	1	2	3	4	5
Spiritual Application:	1	2	3	4	5

EXHIBIT 9
WHAT DOES IT MEAN TO BE A DISCIPLE?

When you boil it down to the basic elements, *intentional male relationships* are forged over the process of discipleship. The principles described in my book *The Spiritual Mentor* spell out in more detail what friendship evangelism looks like.

How many have had questions like:

* Do I periodically experience waves of compassion and empathy for those outside of Christ?

* Do I have some deep friendships with unbelievers?

* Have I had two or more un-churched people in my home in the last month?

* Do I believe God would desire me to be a part of kingdom-building?

* Do I hang around irreligious people?

* Do I really care about those who are unloveable?

* How do I connect with a person on a spiritual level?

* What does it mean to be a disciple?

SIMPLE OVERVIEW

TO KNOW GOD AND MAKE HIM KNOWN

Discipleship is a PROCESS. God's desire is to etch into our lives the imprint of His Son, Jesus. He is responsible for the construction process of making us like Christ. But He needs yielded, available individuals willing to be shaped, molded, and carved by His hands.

Discipleship is apprenticeship. (It is the process of sharing, encouraging, modeling, teaching, listening, and serving—John 1.)

INSTRUCTION MANUAL FOR DISCIPLESHIP
(REFER TO *THE SPIRITUAL MENTOR* BY JIM GRASSI)

✳ Among other things Jesus tells us, "Do not be anxious . . . Be like Me . . . Following Me may cause division . . . Take risks . . . Be shrewd as serpents and innocent as doves" (Matt. 10).

✳ Discipleship is fundamental to our faith and to our relationships (Matt. 4:19).

✳ Discipleship is not about work but about "being" a witness (Acts 1:8).

✳ Simply put, discipleship is friendship with a purpose and spiritual perspective—it is connecting with others (relationship).

EXHIBIT 10
HOW TO START SPIRITUAL CONVERSATIONS

The best way to break into a "spiritual conversation" is to first know their story. Ask questions and seek information about them. Listen carefully, ask questions, show concern, and do *not* be judgmental. Find an area of their life that you can connect with. Maybe it's their work, a former or current illness, trouble in their family, anger issues, coping with doubt, or some other issue.

You should always ask for permission before sharing your faith—"Would you be willing to give me three to five minutes?" or "Could I take a few minutes of your time?" This would be a good way to transition into discussing your testimony and faith.

The following are some ideas for follow-up conversation utilizing the direct method:

* If you'd ever like to know the difference between religion and Christianity, I'd be glad to discuss that question with you.

* Has anyone ever shown you from the Bible how you can know that you're going to heaven?

* Do you ever wonder what happens to you when you die?

The following are some ideas for follow-up conversation utilizing the indirect method:

* Utilize discussions centered on areas like sports, music, nature, hobbies, and so forth.

* Begin conversations with current events or topics that stir passion, like the economy, social issues, war, or the Middle

East. Stay away from topics like politics or specific reference to denominations.

THREE KEYS TO BEING
SUCCESSFUL WITH THE EVENT

✳ Pray fervently that the Holy Spirit will manifest itself in the person. Remember, we are only messengers. It is the Holy Spirit who prepares the heart.

✳ Pique curiosity by being somewhat whimsical and casual. Don't pressure anyone.

✳ Seize split-second opportunities by discussing things that might provoke some "deep thinking" on his part.

EXHIBIT 11
EVENT PLANNING CHECKLIST

SAMPLE EVENT CHECKLISTS

Event: _____

Coordinator: _____

Date: _____ Time: _____

Place: _____

ADMINISTRATION:

- [ ] Objectives defined
- [ ] Post-event integration strategy defined
- [ ] Marketing theme and communication plan defined
- [ ] Full support—staff and congregation
- [ ] Leadership team established
- [ ] Community calendars reviewed for conflicts
- [ ] Prayer initiated
- [ ] Checklists and timelines established
- [ ] Budget developed (if needed)

FACILITY:

- [ ] Contract finalized (if necessary)
- [ ] Liaison person _____
- [ ] Arrangements (tables, chairs, etc.)
- [ ] Sound system and microphones

- [ ] Video projection
- [ ] Heating and cooling

PROGRAM:

- [ ] Speaker/leader_____
- [ ] Equipment needs identified and secured
- [ ] Supplies determined and secured
- [ ] Door prizes
- [ ] Schedule (from opening to closing)
- [ ] Marketing:
- [ ] Media releases (print, radio, TV)
- [ ] Tickets
- [ ] Posters
- [ ] Bulletin inserts
- [ ] Pulpit announcements/drama
- [ ] Mailings
- [ ] Telephone calling
- [ ] Business community
- [ ] Christian community
- [ ] General supplies:
- [ ] Pencils/pens
- [ ] Marking pens
- [ ] Dry erase marker and eraser
- [ ] Paper

- [ ] Survey/response cards
- [ ] Paper clips
- [ ] Stapler
- [ ] Tape (scotch, masking, duct)
- [ ] Scissors/knife
- [ ] String/rope
- [ ] Collection baskets/buckets
- [ ] Cash box and change
- [ ] Food/refreshments:
- [ ] Type/selection
- [ ] Purchase
- [ ] Preparation
- [ ] Serving

PERSONNEL:

- [ ] Section/department leaders
- [ ] Setup
- [ ] Takedown/cleanup
- [ ] Greeters
- [ ] Table leaders/prayer warriors
- [ ] Helpers/assistants
- [ ] Marketing
- [ ] Miscellaneous:
- [ ] Parking

☐ Decorations and displays

☐ Security

☐ Products (books, pamphlets, brochures, video and cassette tapes, etc.)

☐ Photography/video

EXHIBIT 12
THE MARKETING PLAN

(EXECUTIVE SUMMARY)

Having established a foundation, examined marketing principles, and reviewed general marketing considerations, the final act is pulling everything together to formulate a simple marketing plan. The marketing plan will establish the strategy and course of action to effectively prompt people to attend and participate in the event. Having done the homework, putting together a marketing plan now becomes a "pick and choose" process. As in establishing the foundation, the marketing plan is developed by answering a set of one-word questions: Who? What? Why? When? Where? and How? Samples of representative questions are listed below:

Who?

* To whom is the event and activity information to be targeted?

* Who is going to formulate the marketing plan?

* Who is going to design and prepare marketing materials (press releases, tickets, bulletin inserts, and the like)?

* Who is going to distribute the information (volunteers, church staff and leaders, congregation, contracted company)?

What?

* What forms of marketing will be used to market the event (radio, newspaper, one-on-one contact, direct mail, and the like)?

✳ What information and details will be included in each marketing piece?

Why?

✳ Why is it important to market this activity?

✳ Why is one format for disseminating information better than another?

When?

✳ When does information need to be ready for graphic design?

✳ When does information need to be ready for printing?

✳ When is information to be distributed? (Remember: too soon and people forget; too late and people are busy.)

Where?

✳ Where are marketing materials to be placed (countertop displays, bulletin boards, store fronts, Sunday bulletin, and the like)?

How?

✳ How will event information be distributed to the target audience?

✳ How will marketing materials be delivered to distribution points?

SUMMARY

Effective marketing is important for successful events and activities. If the target audience doesn't know what is going on, how are they expected to attend? To formulate and implement an effective marketing plan, one must first establish a foundation on which to build the plan. Next, review and attain a good understanding of sound marketing principles. Third, become familiar with general marketing considerations. It will make marketing a lot easier. Finally, armed with what is learned, put together a simple marketing plan by answering six one-word questions: Who? What? Why? When? Where? and How? And when the plan is established, "Just do it!"

RESOURCES AVAILABLE

Men's Ministry Catalyst: Exhibits from this book and other resources are available by contacting MMC, www.mensministrycatalyst.org or by calling (208) 457-9619.

Weekly Devotionals for Men: Ideal for pastors and men's leaders to e-mail to their men.

http://www.mensministrycatalyst.org/stay-informed/devotional-archives/

MMC Library of Best Practices: Especially designed to assist leaders, available at (208) 762-9216.

MMC Hotline (208) 762-9216: Call anytime for assistance on creating ministry to men.

Monthly Men's Ministry Newsletter: This monthly e-mail newsletter gives you tips and techniques of how to equip, inspire, and motivate men for kingdom purposes, available at www.mensministrycatalyst.org.

SOCIAL MEDIA

http://www.mensministrycatalyst.org/blog

http://www.facebook.com/MensMinistryCatalyst

http://twitter.com/MensMinCatalyst

http://www.youtube.com/user/MensMinCatalyst

Personal Church Consulting: We will send a church consultant to your location; call (208) 762-9216.

Men's Ministry Assessment Survey: We have the capacity to customize, process, and evaluate your survey.

Conferences and Retreats: Our extensive experience in providing speakers, logistics, and support for your men's retreats, conferences, and special events. Call (925) 362-3340.

Speakers Bureau: A list of qualified national speakers and sports personalities to enhance your programs. Call (208) 762-9216.

Church Security: In conjunction with Center Target Sports, we can provide recommendations on church security and safety programs. Call (208) 773-2331.

Primary Provider of Iron Sharpens Iron Programs on the West Coast: (925) 362-3340.

NOTES

INTRODUCTION

1. "America's Families and Living Arrangements: 2012," U.S. Census Bureau, http://www.census.gov/hhes/families/data/cps2012.html, accessed June 21, 2013.
2. Warren W. Wiersbe, *The Bible Exposition Commentary* (Wheaton, IL: Victor Books, 1996), 54.

CHAPTER 1

1. Pat Morley, *The Man in the Mirror* (Grand Rapids: Zondervan, 1997), 70.
2. Steve Farrar, *Anchor Man* (Nashville: Thomas Nelson, 1997), 23, 95.
3. Patrick Morley, *Pastoring Men* (Chicago: Moody Publishers, 2009), 20.
4. Bob Horner, Ron Ralston, and David Sunde, *The Promise Keeper at Work* (Nashville: Thomas Nelson, 2005), 103.
5. Steve Sonderman, *How to Build a Life-Changing Men's Ministry* (Minneapolis, MN: Bethany House Publishers, 1996), 13–31.
6. George Barna, *The Frog in the Kettle* (Ventura, CA: Regal, 1990), 138.
7. Robert Lewis, *The Church of Irresistible Influence* (Grand Rapids: Zondervan, 2001), 24, 29–30, 31.
8. "Why Men Matter—Both Now and Forever," Washington Area Coalition of Men's Ministries, www.wacmm.org/stats.html, accessed October 14, 2013.
9. George Barna, *Revolution* (Carol Stream, IL: Tyndale House Publishers, 2005), 105.
10. Neil Brown, "The Compelling Case for a New Model of Men's Ministry," Adventures in Men's Ministry, http://neilbrown.blogspot.com/2009/01/compelling-case-for-new-model-of-mens.html, accessed October 14, 2013.
11. Ibid.
12. John Eldredge, *Wild at Heart* (Nashville: Thomas Nelson, 2001), 5.
13. Patrick Morley, *Pastoring Men* (Chicago: Moody Publishers, 2008), 47.

CHAPTER 2

1. The Weather Channel, www.weather.com/newscenter/ topstories/060829katrinastats.html, August 21, 2009, accessed August 1, 2013.
2. For more information on this distinction, see my previous book in this series, *The Spiritual Mentor* (Nashville: Thomas Nelson, 2013).
3. *The New Shorter Oxford English Dictionary*, Lesley Brown, ed. (Oxford: Clarendon Press, 1993).
4. We will further address the concept of "relational platforms" in a later chapter.
5. Pat Morley, *Pastoring Men* (Chicago: Moody Publishers, 2009), 78.
6. Jim Grassi, *The Spiritual Mentor* (Nashville: Thomas Nelson, 2013).
7. See Mike Genung, "Current Porn Statistics," The Road to Grace, http://www.roadtograce.net/current-porn-statistics, accessed October 14, 2013.

CHAPTER 3

1. Marine Corps News Room, "Medal of Honor Citation for Cpl. Jason L. Dunham," http://www.marine-corps-news.com/2007/01/medal_of_honor_citation_for_cp.htm, accessed October 14, 2013.
2. Preston Gillham, *Things Only Men Know: What Matters Most in the Life of a Man* (Eugene, OR: Harvest House Publishers, 1999), 49–50.
3. John Ortberg, *If You Want to Walk on Water, You've Got to Get Out of the Boat* (Grand Rapids: Zondervan, 2000), 24.
4. David Jeremiah, *Facing the Giants in Your Life: Study Guide* (86) (Turning Point, 2001).

CHAPTER 4

1. Michiko Kakutani, "Muscle Memory: The Training of Navy SEALs Commandos," *New York Times*, May 8, 2011.
2. Ibid.
3. Team Building Techniques.com, http://www.team-building-techniques.com/benefits-of-teamwork.html, accessed August 1, 2013.

CHAPTER 5

1. Tamara Lush, "Most of Fla. House over Sinkhole Demolished," *The Associated Press*, March 3, 2013, http://bigstory.ap.org/article/rescuers-end-effort-find-body-fla-sinkhole
2. David Murrow, *Why Men Hate Going to Church* (Nashville: Thomas Nelson, 2005), 5–8.
3. Bob Horner, Ron Ralston, and David Sunde, *The Promise Keeper at Work* (Nashville: Thomas Nelson, 2005), 103.
4. David Murrow, *Why Men Hate Going to Church* (Nashville: Thomas Nelson, 2005), 5–8.

CHAPTER 6

1. "In the same way that iron sharpens iron, a person sharpens the character of his friend" (Prov. 27:17 The Voice).

CHAPTER 7

1. "America's Families and Living Arrangements: 2012," U.S. Census Bureau, http://www.census.gov/hhes/families/data/cps2012.html, accessed June 21, 2013.

CHAPTER 8

1. Tim Wright, "Why I Believe the Church May Be the Best Hope for Our Boys," CNN iReport, ireport.cnn.com/docs/DOC-976165, accessed May 22, 2013.
2. Ibid.
3. Amanda L. Chan, "Going to Church Linked with Better Mood, Study Finds," The Huffington Post, http://www.huffingtonpost.com/2012/03/25/going-to-church-mood-positive-emotions-well-being_n_1375707.html?ref=religion&ir=Religion, accessed October 14, 2013.
4. Dr. Chuck Stecker, interview with the author on June 10, 2013.
5. Ibid.
6. Contact www.fathersinthefield.com 307-332-0901.

CHAPTER 9

1. B. A. Robinson, Ontario Consultants on Religious Tolerance, *The Barna Report*, July 20, 2009. Barna uses the term "non-denominational" to refer to Evangelical Christian congregations that are not affiliated with a specific denomination. The vast majority are fundamentalist in their theological beliefs.
2. Donald Hughes, quoted in Ebenezer Gyasi, *Spiritual Marriage: The Curse of Illicit Sexual Union* (Bloomington, IN: AuthorHouse, 2006), 9.
3. Sarah Womack, "Modern Men Feel Emasculated, Study Claims," *The Telegraph*, http://www.telegraph.co.uk/news/uknews/1582863/Modern-men-feel-emasculated-study-claims.html.
4. The Archdiocese of Kansas City in Kansas, Freedom from Pornography: Awareness, http://www.archkck.org/eyefreedom_awareness_full, accessed October 14, 2013 .
5. Kurt Smith, "Top 3 Causes of Addiction to Porn," http://www.guystuffcounseling.com/counseling-men-blog/bid/47051/Top-3-Causes-of-Addiction-to-Porn.
6. Rebecca Grace, Focus on the Family Poll, October 2003, Quoted in "When Dad Falls." *American Family Association Journal* Web. 25 September 2004. http://www.afajournal.org/2004/september/904WhenDadFalls.asp, accessed January 3, 2014.
7. http://www.divorcewizards.com/Divorce-Statistics-Pornography.html.
8. "Why Religion Matters: The Impact of Religious Practice on Social Stability," *The Heritage Foundation Backgrounder*, 1064, 25 January, 1996.
9. Mike Strobbe, The Associated Press, May 2, 2013. Quoted in http://www.newsday.com/news/health/u-s-suicide-rate-rose-sharply-among-middle-aged-1.5187010. Accessed January 3, 2014.

CHAPTER 10

1. Jacqueline Olds and Richard S. Schwartz, *The Lonely American: Drifting Apart in the Twenty-First Century* (Boston: Beacon Press, 2010), from the book description, http://www.amazon.com/Lonely-American-Drifting-Twenty-first-Century/dp/0807000353.
2. Charles Swindoll, *Devotions for Growing Strong in the Seasons of Life* (Grand Rapids: Zondervan, 1983), 406.

3. Dale Carnegie, *How to Win Friends and Influence People* (New York: Simon & Schuster, Inc., 2010), 52.

CHAPTER 11

1. *Braveheart*, Dir. Mel Gibson, Paramount, 1995.
2. Roger Oswald, *Sports Ministry Binder* (San Jose, CA: Church Sports International, 2003), 94.
3. Vince D'Acchioli, New Life Men Whitepaper, On Target Ministries, 2008.

CHAPTER 13

1. Sue Valerian, "Why Non-Profits Need Content Marketing," Content Marketing World, http://contentmarketingworld.com/news/why-non-profits-need-content-marketing/, accessed October 14, 2013.

ACKNOWLEDGEMENTS

1. William J. Bennett, *The Book of Virtues* (New York: Simon and Schuster, 1993), 335.

BIBLIOGRAPHY

Aldrich, Joseph C. *Gentle Persuasion*. Portland, OR: Multnomah Press, 1988.

Arnold, J. Heinrich. *Discipleship*. Farmington, PA: Plough Publishing House, 2007.

_____. *Life-Style Evangelism*. Portland, OR: Multnomah Press, 1981.

_____. *Living Proof*. Colorado Springs, CO: NavPress, 1989.

Bennett, William J. *The Book of Virtues*. New York: Simon and Schuster, 1993.

Bonhoeffer, Dietrich. *The Cost of Discipleship*. New York: Macmillan Publishing Co., 1963.

Boreham, F. W. *The Uttermost Star*. London: Epworth Press, 1935.

Coleman, Robert E. *The Master Plan of Evangelism*. Grand Rapids: Fleming H. Revell, 1993.

Downer, Phil. *Eternal Impact*. Eugene, OR: Harvest House Publishers, 1997.

Hull, Bill. *Jesus Christ, Disciple Maker*. Grand Rapids: Fleming H. Revell, 1990.

Jones, E. Stanley. *How to Pray*. Nashville: Abingdon Press, 1979.

Logos Bible Software. *Logos*. Bellington, WA: Logos Bible Software.

MacDonald, Gordon. *Ordering Your Private World*. Nashville: Thomas Nelson Publishers, 1985.

_____. *Restoring Your Spiritual Passion*. Nashville: Thomas Nelson Publishers, 1986.

Morley, Patrick. *Pastoring Men*. Chicago, IL: Moody Publishers, 2009.

_____. *No Man Left Behind*. Chicago, IL: Moody Publishers, 2006.

Needham, David C. *Close to His Majesty*. Portland, OR: Multnomah Press, 1987.

Nun, Mendel. *The Sea of Galilee and Its Fishermen in the New Testament*. Ein Gev, Israel: Kibbutz Ein Gev Publishing, 1989.

Ogilvie, Lloyd J. *Making Stress Work for You*. Waco, TX: Word, 1984.

Petersen, Jim. *Lifestyle Discipleship*. Colorado Springs, CO: NavPress, 1993.

————. *Living Proof*. Colorado Springs, CO: NavPress, 1989.

Phillips, J. B. *Your God Is Too Small*. New York: Macmillan Publishing Co., 1961.

Putman, Jim. *Real-Life Discipleship*. Colorado Springs, CO: NavPress, 2010.

Putman, Willis, Guindon, Krause. *Real-Life Discipleship Training Manual*. Colorado Springs, CO: NavPress, 2010.

Richards, Lawrence O. *The 365-Day Devotional Commentary*. Wheaton, IL: Victor Books, 1931.

Stecker, Chuck. *Anchor Points Seminar Booklet*. Littleton, CO: A Chosen Generation, 2007.

Swindoll, Charles R. *Discipleship—Bible Study Guide*. Fullerton, CA: Insight for Living, 1990.

————. *Laugh Again*. Waco, TX: Word, 1991.

Thayer, Joseph Henry. *Greek-English Lexicon of the New Testament*. New York:

Harper Brothers Publishers, 1899.

ABOUT THE AUTHOR

Dr. Jim Grassi is an award-winning author, communicator, out-doorsman, pastor, and former television co-host. He has presented hundreds of messages and programs around the world that helped equip people to fulfill the Great Commission (Matt. 28). He brings a sense of challenge, wisdom, excitement, and humor to his presentations, as he connects with people of various cultures and backgrounds. Through his multimedia outreach ministry, he encourages participants toward a greater understanding and appreciation of evangelism, discipleship, and the development of creating vibrant men's ministries. His practical approach to teaching biblical truth has captivated audiences around the world.

Jim Grassi is the founder and president of the culturally strategic Men's Ministry Catalyst, an organization he incorporated in 1981. Grassi is also the recognized author of several books, including *The Ultimate Fishing Challenge, Heaven on Earth, In Pursuit of the Prize, The Ultimate Hunt, Crunch Time, A Study Guide of Israel, The Ultimate Men's Ministry Encyclopedia, Crunch Time in the Red Zone, Gut's, Grace, and Glory—A Football Devotional*, and *The Spiritual Mentor*. Jim has also written numerous magazine articles, booklets, and tracts.

Grassi was born and reared in the San Francisco Bay area. Known for his evangelistic heart, he teaches people from a background of an outdoorsman, public administrator, Hall of Fame fisherman, college professor, businessman, community leader, and pastor. He has served in the capacity of a chaplain with the San Francisco 49ers, the Oakland Raiders, Hurricane Katrina, and the Post Falls Idaho Police Department. His life experiences, study of discipleship, and work with hundreds of churches has given him a unique perspective on helping men to know God and make Him known.

KNOW YOURSELF, HONOR OTHERS, LIVE FOR CHRIST

CHECK OUT THE OTHER BOOKS IN THE SERIES

THE SPIRITUAL MENTOR

JIM GRASSI

MORE THAN A FISHERMAN

JIM GRASSI

FINISHING WELL FINISHING STRONG

JIM GRASSI

Now Available

Available June 2014

Available September 2014

Discover what it means to live for Christ. Learn how to fully surrender yourself over to God. Rescue not only your faith, but also others.

THOMAS NELSON
Since 1798